THE NEXT STEP IN CONSCIOUS EVOLUTION

THE NEXT STEP IN CONSCIOUS EVOLUTION

BEYOND THE DARK SHADOWS OF TRANSHUMANISM TOWARDS AN EVOLUTIONARY SPIRITUALITY

A TRIBUTE TO BARBARA MARX HUBBARD

• • •

From Conscious Evolution 1.0 to Conscious Evolution 2.0

One Mountain, Many Paths: Oral Essays
Volume Sixteen

DR. MARC GAFNI AND BARBARA MARX HUBBARD

Copyright © 2025 Center for World Philosophy and Religion

All Rights Reserved

No part of this book may be used or reproduced in any manner whatsoever without written permission except in the case of brief quotations embodied in critical articles or reviews.

No part of this book may be reproduced, or stored in a retrieval system, or transmitted in any form or by any means, electronic, mechanical, photocopying, recording, or otherwise, without express written permission of the publisher.

All brand names and product names used in this book are trademarks, registered trademarks, or trade names of their respective holders.

For additional information and press releases please contact CWPR Publishing.

Author: Marc Gafni and Barbara Marx Hubbard
Title: The Next Step in Conscious Eovlution
From Conscious Evolution 1.0 to Conscious Evolution 2.0

Identifiers: ISBN 979-8-88834-096-7 (electronic)
ISBN 979-8-88834-095-0 (paperback)

Edited by Elena-Maslova-Levin, Timothy Paul Aryeh, Paul Bennett, Carol Bennett Dorothea Betz, and Krista Josepha Steenbergen

World Philosophy and Religion Press, St. Johnsbury, VT
in conjunction with

IP Integral Publishers

https://worldphilosophyandreligion.org

JOIN THE REVOLUTION!

CONTENTS

EDITORIAL NOTE ABOUT AUTHORSHIP, EDITING, AND THE RADICAL CONTEXT FOR THIS SERIES   XIII

LOVE OR DIE: LOCATING OURSELVES   XXV

ABOUT THIS VOLUME   XLII

CHAPTER 1   **CELEBRATING BARBARA MARX HUBBARD: THE PROMISE WILL BE KEPT**

Celebrating Barbara's 91st Birthday	1
We're in Celebration, and in Our Celebration Is All of The Pain and All of the Joy	4
We Need Line and Circle Qualities at Higher Levels of Consciousness	5
Evolutionary Love Code: You Are A Unique Set of Allurements	8
Success 1.0, Success 2.0, Success 3.0	9
Prayer Affirms the Personhood of Cosmos	10
The Wheel of Co-Creation 1.0	12
The Wheel of Co-Creation 2.0	13
Evolutionary Intelligence Equals Desire	16
Deepest Heart's Desire and the DNA of an Emerging Culture	18
I Don't Grow Older, I Grow Newer	21
Barbara Ran for Evolution	22

CHAPTER 2   THE CONTINUITY OF CONSCIOUSNESS: DEATH IS NOT THE END OF THE STORY

We Respond to the First and Second Shocks of Existence	25
Barbara Is With Us in the Continuity of Consciousness	27
The Movement to Resurrection	29
After the Crucifixion, There's Always Resurrection	30
No Matter What Is Going on in My Life, I Trust With Complete Trust	32
Evolutionary Love Code: Death and Resurrection Are Natural Expressions of the Intimate Pattern of Reality	33
That's Us, on the Road to the Planetary Awakening in Love	34
This Is the Real Thing—We Live Beyond Death	36
Eight Doors of Understanding to the Continuity of Consciousness	39
Door One: The Door of Longing	40
Door Two: The Fear of Nothingness Is That Which Is Beyond Nothingness	41
Door Three: The Eternal Quality of Timeless Time and Placeless Place	42
Door Four: Intuition of Justice and Fairness	43
Door Five: The Knowing of the Hero	44
Door Six: The Experience of Unique Self	47
Door Seven: Either Everything's Meaningful Or Nothing's Meaningful	48
Door Eight: The Experience of Loving Is the Experience Of Eternity	49

CHAPTER 3   WHY LEVELS OF CONSCIOUSNESS MATTER: THE GREAT STORY OF EVOLUTIONARY DEVOTION

The New Story of Value Is Our New Home	53
Every Human Being Has the Right to Desire and to Be Desired	55

Evolutionary Love Code: Wake Up, Grow Up, Show Up	56
The Field of Intelligence Hears You Talking	57
The Purpose of Reality Is to Wake Up and to Grow Up	59
Wake Up States Are Not Enough	60
Developmental Levels of Clare Graves	64
The Experience of Commitment at Different Levels of Consciousness	68
"Become A Member" Means Something Different at Each Level of Consciousness	70
From Tier One to Tier Two	71
The Jump From First Tier to Second Tier	72

CHAPTER 4   CELEBRATING THE COURAGE TO EVOLVE: BEYOND THE DARK SHADOWS OF TRANSHUMANISM AND EVOLUTIONARY SPIRITUALITY

Celebrating Barbara Marx Hubbard: the Ability to Keep Evolving and Transforming	77
Celebrating 300 Weeks of *One Mountain, Many Paths*: Humans Are Wildly Good, True and Beautiful	81
To Give Up Being Right Is Being *Homo Amor*	85
The Evolution of Love Says *No* to Eugenics	91
The Techno-Utopian Vision Needs to Be Grounded in Unique Self	94
Evolutionary Love Code: Moving Beyond Demonization	98
Incarnating the Impulse of Evolution: Barbara's First Sermon in *Evolutionary Church*	98
Evolutionary Chakra Meditation	99
Leaving the Personal Behind Leads to Totalitarianism	103
Story as Prayer: Authentic Mystical Ecstasy Never Ignores the Hunger of Even One Individual	106

CHAPTER 5   CELEBRATING THE COURAGE TO EVOLVE: BEYOND THAT DARK SHADOWS OF TRANSHUMANISM AND EVOLUTIONARY SPIRITUALITY, PART 2

Joining of Genius	111
The Second Shock of Existence: the Death of Our Humanity	112
Conscious Evolution and the Wheel of Co-Creation	114
The Shadow of Evolutionary Spirituality and Transhumanism	115
Without Articulating First Principles and First Values, You Cannot Arouse Outrage	120
Modeling Evolutionary Conversations	122
Subtle Mccarthyism and Fear on the Internet	126
The Irreducible Infinite Value of Unique Personhood	130
Conversation Absent First Principles and First Values Is Impossible	132
Tech Plex Creativity Needs to Participate in the New Story Of Value	135

CHAPTER 6   BARBARA MARX HUBBARD'S BIRTHDAY: THE EVOLUTION OF CONSCIOUS EVOLUTION

Are You Ready to Awaken as Conscious Evolution?	139
We Need Infrastructure to Articulate the New World Philosophy and Religion	144
Barbara Marx Hubbard Engaged Life With Full Passion Every Day	145
Integrating Barbara's Legacy Into the New Story of Value	147
Conscious Evolution 1.0	148
Conscious Evolution 2.0: I Am Conscious Evolution in Person	153
Next Steps Towards Conscious Evolution 2.0	157

CHAPTER 7	THE EVOLUTION OF CONSCIOUS EVOLUTION: CELEBRATING BARBARA MARX HUBBARD, MY EVOLUTIONARY WHOLE MATE

Re-Visioning Conscious Evolution   159

Evolution Is the Synergy of Radical *Telos* and Complete Freedom   161

Plotlines of Evolution Awakening in Us   164

The Way We Meet Barbara Is by Showing Up in Our Full Selves   166

APPENDIX: SONGS   **168**

INDEX   **172**

ABOUT THE AUTHORS   **180**

EDITORIAL NOTE ABOUT AUTHORSHIP, EDITING, AND THE RADICAL CONTEXT FOR THIS SERIES

ORAL ESSAYS FROM THE ONE MOUNTAIN, MANY PATHS WEEKLY BROADCAST

This volume is part of the Oral Essays library, a series of lightly edited, compiled transcripts of oral teachings given by Dr. Marc Gafni and the late Barbara Marx Hubbard in their weekly online broadcast, *One Mountain, Many Paths*, which they co-founded in 2017. Originally called an "Evolutionary Church," *One Mountain, Many Paths* became a key venue for the articulation of an inspired and deeply grounded new Story of Value in response to the meta-crisis. Marc and Barbara—together with Zak Stein,[1] Kristina Kincaid, Ken Wilber, Sally Kempton, Lori Galperin, Aubrey Marcus and dozens of other thought-leaders over the years—began to articulate what they call a World Philosophy and World Religion[2] as a context for our diversity.

---

[1] Zak, together with Ken Wilber, has been Marc's primary intellectual partner and an initiate lineage holder in CosmoErotic Humanism.

[2] This project is grounded in four core organizational frameworks: 1) The Center for World Philosophy and Religion, co-founded by Marc Gafni, Zachary Stein, Sally Kempton, and Ken Wilber, and chaired over the years by John P. Mackey, Barbara Marx Hubbard, Aubrey Marcus, Gabrielle Anwar and Shareef Malnik, Carrie Kish and Adam Bellow, and Kathleen J. Brownback. 2) The Office for the Future, chaired by Stephanie Valcke and Ivan Bossyut. 3) The World Philosophy and Religion Press, founded and chaired by Aubrey Marcus, together with Marc Gafni and Zachary Stein. 4) The Foundation for Conscious Evolution, founded by Barbara Marx Hubbard and currently chaired by Peter Fiekowsky. For a complete list of key leadership, see the Office for the Future website, www.officeforthefuture.com.

THE NEXT STEP IN CONSCIOUS EVOLUTION

Until Barbara's passing in 2019, she and Marc transmitted teachings together as evolutionary partners and "whole mates," weaving together insights and transmissions from their decades of practice, study, teaching, and activism into a synergy of wisdom, a grounded vision for future policy across all sectors of society.

Much of the *dharma* material below comes directly from Marc, so it was originally all in quotation marks—but that looked a little odd. So per his suggestion we removed them, and the reader should consider the paragraphs on the next several pages as one extended quote from him. We are joyfully grateful to Marc for the clarity of his *dharma*, the elegance and "second simplicity" of this language, and the mad, Outrageous Love with which he transmits his teachings.

Barbara and Marc called the mission of *One Mountain* "a Planetary Awakening in Evolutionary Love Through Unique Self Symphonies." We are an evolutionary community with a deeply grounded, radically alive, and "post-tragic" revolutionary spirit. We are activating a new humanity and awakening as a new species: *Homo amor*, the fulfillment of *Homo sapiens*.

One Mountain is committed to articulating a Story of Value that can become the ground for the new society that must be birthed in response to the meta-crisis. We recognize that we are living at a pivotal moment in history. In this "time between stories," the great moral imperative is to tell the new Story of Value. It is ours to do, personally and collectively, with great trembling and ecstatic joy.

FROM DOGMA TO DHARMA: ETERNAL AND EVOLVING FIRST PRINCIPLES AND FIRST VALUES

The teachings are grounded in decades of deep study across many wisdom traditions. Over the years, week by week, these teachings were incrementally developed within the framework of the *One Mountain, Many Paths* broadcast. We often refer to these teachings as *dharma*.

EDITORIAL NOTE

This word was originally used in lineage traditions to refer to something like universal law. This is a crucial realization: just as there is universal law in mathematical value, there is also a sense of universal law in ethics and value.

Historically, *dharma* often devolved into unchanging dogma. Evolution was ignored, and the natural process of *dharma* evolution became disconnected from its deep, eternal context. The weakness of the word *dharma* is that too often it did not include the evolving insights of the sciences, it confused local cultural truths with universal truths, and it used words like "eternal," as in "eternal Tao," as opposed to words like "evolution."

Eternal came to mean unchanging, and that kind of thinking often led to overly ethnocentric readings of *dharma*. Local systems would claim their religious and cultural insights as immutable, which stood in the way of the emergence of a genuine world Story of Value that is real, inherent to Cosmos, and backed by the Universe—even as it is also always evolving.

Or, as we often say, "eternal value is evolving value. The eternal Tao is the evolving Tao."

We have shown that, emergent from profound insights in the "interior sciences," eternal does not mean unchanging in time; it means what we call the deeper Field of ErosValue that is beneath culture, geography, and history, which lives beneath all individual and collective values, and beneath time and space itself.

As such, we have gradually transitioned from the term *dharma* to the term *Value*, in the sense of the Field of Value that lives beneath all values. This Field of Value discloses as First Principles and First Values embedded in a Story of Value.

Indeed, as the interior sciences knew and the exterior sciences imply, Reality arises in a Field of ErosValue in which an entire set of mathematical, musical, molecular, moral, and mystical values are the very ground of all being. That Field of Value is eternal—the true ground of the Good, True and Beautiful—even as it is evolving.

But of course, it is equally critical not just to talk about evolving value, but to ground the evolving value in its true nature, the eternal Field of First Principles and First Values, always reaching for ever-more life, ever-more love, ever-more care, ever-more depth, ever-more uniqueness, ever-more intimate communion, and ever-more transformation.

As such, when we refer to the word *dharma*, which still appears in these texts together with the word value, we refer to an evolving *dharma* grounded in an *eternal and evolving* Field of Value. Indeed, eternity and evolution are two faces of the whole, opposites joined at the hip, that characterize the nature of our Cosmos in virtually all of its expressions.

It's in these terms that we ground a robust world philosophy that integrates the validated, leading-edge insights of premodern traditional wisdom, modern wisdom, and more recent postmodern insights, weaving them together into a new whole greater than the sum of its parts.

This new whole is a shared Story of Value rooted in First Principles and First Values that are both eternal and evolving.

These First Principles and First Values of Cosmos are woven together into a new Story of Value as a context for our diversity, a new Universe Story. This new Story gives us the best possible responses we have to the mystery, and to the great questions:

- Who am I? Who are we?
- Where am I? Where are we?
- What should I do? What should we do?

It is only through such a shared Universe Story—a narrative of identity and ethos as a context for our blessed diversity—that we can realize how what unites is so much greater than what divides us.

EDITORIAL NOTE

Only a new Story of Value will allow us to both respond to the meta-crisis and participate together in birthing the most true, good, and beautiful world that we already know is possible.

THIS ORAL ESSAYS SERIES IS AN ENTRYWAY TO THE GREAT LIBRARY OF COSMOEROTIC HUMANISM

This Oral Essays series is part of the overarching project of the Great Library at the Center for World Philosophy and Religion, led by Dr. Marc Gafni, together with Dr. Zak Stein. The aim of the Great Library project is to articulate a robust and comprehensive new Story of Value, CosmoErotic Humanism, in the form of dozens of well-researched and extensively footnoted academic works.

Our vision is to provide the philosophical framework that will be vital for navigating humanity through this time of immense crisis and transformation.

To begin your journey into CosmoErotic Humanism, we tenderly refer you to the book *First Principles and First Values*, co-authored by Marc Gafni, Zak Stein, and Ken Wilber, under the name David J. Temple. David J. Temple is a pseudonym created for enabling ongoing collaborative authorship at the Center for World Philosophy and Religion. The two primary authors behind David J. Temple are Marc Gafni and Zak Stein, and for different projects, specific writers will be named as part of the collaboration, such as Ken Wilber and others.

Three other volumes complete this introduction: *A Return to Eros*, by Marc Gafni and Kristina Kincaid; *Your Unique Self*, by Marc Gafni; and *Education in a Time between Worlds*, by Zak Stein.

We hope that the Oral Essays in this volume, with their informal style of transmission, will serve as an allurement and entryway for you into the more formal books of the Great Library that provide the robust intellectual underpinnings of the new Story of Value.

A NOTE ABOUT THE EDITORS

This Oral Essays collection has been edited by students of the new Story of CosmoErotic Humanism. Each of us has actively participated in *One Mountain, Many Paths*, and most of us have been in deep "Holy of Holies" study with Dr. Marc Gafni for many years.

We have been privileged to find ourselves well-versed in the teachings, and even emerging as lineage-holders of CosmoErotic Humanism.[3]

We view this editing project as a privilege and a deep practice of study and clarification. We experience ourselves as a *mystical editing society*, frequently meeting and conversing together about the content—the depth of knowledge and wisdom offered here—as well as the technical intricacies involved with publishing a beautiful and coherent series of books. In so doing, we function as a "Unique Self Symphony," which itself is a Dharmic

---

[3] CosmoErotic Humanism is a world philosophical movement aimed at reconstructing the collapse of value at the core of global culture. Much like Romanticism or Existentialism, CosmoErotic Humanism is not merely a theory but a movement that changes the very mood of Reality. It is an invitation to participate in evolving the source code of consciousness and culture towards a cosmocentric *ethos* for a planetary civilization.

The term CosmoErotic Humanism, initially coined by Dr. Gafni and colleagues, points to a complex, multi-faceted, layered, and nuanced evolutionary set of insights that has evolved over decades of intensive research, teaching, and spiritual practice from deep within a wide range of wisdom traditions (including the Wisdom of Solomon lineage tradition, Bodhisattva Buddhism, and Kashmir Shaivism), as well as multiple disciplines including complexity theory, chaos theory, emergence theory, molecular biology, and the more classical disciplines of the humanities.

The seeds of CosmoErotic Humanism were planted with Dr. Marc Gafni's work on a two-volume, 1,000-page opus called *Radical Kabbalah* (Integral Publishers, 2012). This scholarly work, sourced from deep study within the esoteric lineage texts of the Wisdom of Solomon, points to a non-dual, or acosmic, realization which—unlike the prevailing conceptualization of non-duality—does not efface the human being; rather, it is highly humanistic in its nature. The next step in the evolution of CosmoErotic Humanism was the insight that all of Reality is evolving Eros, which lives in, as, and through the human being.

A failure of Eros leads inexorably to the creation of narratives of "pseudo-eros." CosmoErotic Humanism is a response to the modern mental and social breakdown sourced in the proliferation of multiple forms of pseudo-eros and its broken narratives, such as rivalrous conflict governed by win/lose metrics and the dogmatic denial of intrinsic value in Cosmos, which together generate our current "global intimacy disorder."

EDITORIAL NOTE

term that connotes an omni-considerate collaboration between realized Unique Selves synergizing our unique gifts into a new emergence greater than the sum of the parts. Even as we worked diligently to standardize our editing styles, meeting on a weekly basis to debate the nuances of phrasing, we also operated from within a deep appreciation of the unique style that each editor brought to his or her work. As such, the reader might notice some variation in editing style among the books.

Please note that Dr. Marc Gafni has not reviewed these edited Oral Essays, as he is deeply engaged in writing the formal books of the Great Library. But he has been generous in responding to questions and providing overall guidance in the project. Overall, as Marc's students and students of the *dharma*, we have made it a key project at the Center to publish these pieces of work relatively independently.

OUR UNIQUE ORAL-ESSAY EDITING STYLE PRESERVES THE ENERGY OF THE ORIGINAL TRANSMISSION

Dr. Marc Gafni is a uniquely gifted teacher whose oral transmission is imbued with a quality that has proven transformative for his students. Many of us feel mystically transformed by both the content and the underlying energy of the transmission style. Therefore, as we like to say, *trust the magic ways the dharma comes through your unique understanding!*

As Marc's empowered students, colleagues, and beloved friends, we have a deep knowing that these teachings are vital for the survival and thriving of humanity as we know it, and we recognize the importance of publishing his teachings in a written format that will be accessible by future generations. At the same time, we sought to preserve the Eros of the original oral transmission with all of its nuance, power, and depth. Our intention in the editing process, to the greatest extent possible, has been to keep these spoken artifacts intact in order to maintain the flow of the original transmission. We have therefore chosen not to engage in intensive formal editing, as we found that doing so resulted in the loss of the energetic transmission that is so key to fully receiving the *dharma*.

After experimenting with many ways to present these texts, we developed a specific way of laying out the text on the page. Marc, in collaboration with Zak Stein and Russian intellectual/artist Elena Maslova-Levin—and ultimately all of the editors, through many conversations—developed a unique, artistic presentation of the text, using bolding, italics, bullet points, and other stylistic features which together serve to accentuate the immediacy of the oral transmission.

As part of this editing style, intended to preserve the integrity of the original transmission, we have refrained from removing the frequent recapitulations of key themes. We found that each recapitulation contributes something vital to the rhythm and music beneath the words, like the beating drum of our hearts. These recapitulations not only review previous material but also add important new emphases, perspectives, and elements of the new Story of Value. We ask for your patience as a reader to trust the rhythm of these texts, and we trust you as a reader to have the depth and steadiness to find your way through.

KEY COMPONENTS: LINK TO THE ORIGINAL BROADCAST, EVOLUTIONARY LOVE CODES AND PRAYER

To supplement the written word, each episode includes a QR code linking to the original broadcast on YouTube, as well as occasional links to featured songs and video clips.

Each episode also centers around an "Evolutionary Love Code," formulated by Marc. These codes are part of the ongoing articulation and distillation of the *dharma* as it unfolds and emerges, week by week, over the course of many years, through the mystical process we call Outrageous Love or Evolutionary Love.

EDITORIAL NOTE

Another core component of the *One Mountain, Many Paths* episodes is what Marc and Barbara called "Evolutionary Prayer." Prayer is experienced in *One Mountain* not in the old fundamentalist sense of a "cosmic vending-machine god" who is alienated from Cosmos. Marc refers to this as the "god you do not and should not believe in"—and he often adds, "the god you don't believe in does not exist."

GOD IS THE INFINITE INTIMATE

In fact, in the *dharma* of CosmoErotic Humanism, a new name for God has emerged: the "Infinite Intimate," who appears in first-, second-, and third-person expressions. Marc first shared this name as he heard it whispered in 2023, although earlier intimations and formulations of the name appeared as early as 2010.

In first person, God is infinitely alive and as intimate as our own first-person experience.

In second person, God is the infinitely intimate Personhood of Cosmos that knows our name and holds us—the God about whom we say, *whenever we fall, we fall into Her hands*. This is the God who is our Beloved, Father, Mother, Lover, and Evolutionary Partner.

Finally, in third person, God inheres in all of the First Principles and First Values of Cosmos, and in the laws of science (both interior and exterior) that govern manifest Reality.

Therefore, we have a realization of God as not only the Infinity of Power but also the Infinity of Intimacy.

In *One Mountain, Many Paths*, we are reclaiming prayer at a higher level of consciousness. And we are reclaiming prayer as deep, alive, loving, and intimate conversations with God as the Infinite Intimate who knows our name.

THE NEXT STEP IN CONSCIOUS EVOLUTION

REFLECTING ON THE CO-CREATION BETWEEN DR. MARC GAFNI AND BARBARA MARX HUBBARD

Barbara and Marc met five years before Barbara passed. As Barbara said so often, "before I met Marc, I was sure that I was done." Barbara had taught so beautifully for decades, focusing particularly on a powerful articulation of "conscious evolution." Indeed, it would not be inaccurate to say that Barbara was the greatest storyteller of conscious evolution of her time.

Conscious evolution was also a premise in Marc's thinking, but drawn from an entirely different set of sources and experiences. Barbara drew from the classical sources of evolutionary spirituality, such as Teilhard de Chardin, Buckminster Fuller, and many others. Indeed, she was closely associated with Fuller, and was perhaps de Chardin's most ardent intellectual devotee.

Marc drew a somewhat different vision of conscious evolution from the interior sciences of the great wisdom traditions, with a primary emphasis on what he refers to as the "Solomon lineages," merged together with careful readings of the leading edges of the sciences.

In the old version of conscious evolution, the movement from unconscious to conscious was a movement of evolution by chance to evolution by choice.

Together Marc and Barbara evolved the old version of Conscious Evolution, pointing out that evolution itself was always in some sense conscious, but as Marc formulated it, the awakening to conscious evolution refers to the awakening of evolution as human consciousness, coupled with the human realization of being conscious evolution in person, and the human capacity to locate oneself within the context of the larger evolutionary story.

Marc focused his attention on an entirely different dimension of Reality, which he and his colleagues began to call CosmoErotic Humanism. The Intimate Universe, Homo amor, Unique Self and Unique Self Symphonies, God as the Infinity of Intimacy, Eros and the CosmoErotic Universe, distinctions like Role Mate, Soul Mate and Whole Mate, the Four Selves,

EDITORIAL NOTE

Evolutionary Love, Outrageous Love, Evolution: the Love Story of the Universe, First Principles and First Values, Evolving Perennialism, the Evolution of Love, and many more are terms articulated by Gafni and shared with Barbara in their conversation, study, and creative engagement.

Some terms they coined together, for example "a Planetary Awakening in Love through Unique Self Symphonies," where Gafni described Unique Self Symphonies, and Barbara aligned her vision of a planetary Pentecost to Marc's vision of Unique Self Symphonies.

Other key terms were unique and articulated by Barbara, for example: conscious evolution, teleros, telerotic, from joining genes to joining genius, regenopause, vocational arousal, birthing of humanity, synergy engine, and of course her work around what she called the Wheel of Co-creation.

Ultimately, Marc and Barbara attempted to synergize their work in what they called the Wheel of Co-creation 2.0. Barbara and Marc experienced themselves as merging their respective *dharma* into what they began to refer to as Conscious Evolution 2.0, or later, CosmoErotic Humanism.

The first 129 episodes of One Mountain, Many Paths took place in the last period of Barbara's life and reflect the depth and texture of the stunning evolutionary whole-mate meeting between her and Marc.

As Barbara was deep in study with Marc, a lot of what she shared in Evolutionary Church was the *dharma* of their deep study and collaboration.

Although sometimes it may be clear who is speaking, we generally publish these early episodes in what we are calling "one voice." The first 129 episodes, with Marc and Barbara together, have been grouped chronologically. Episodes 130 to 400 and onwards, which were transmitted by Marc, have been grouped by topic.

THE INVITATION

We invite you to find your way into this revolution. Each one of our Unique Selves and unique gifts are desperately needed as we co-create this new Story of Value together, as part of the covenant between generations, for the sake of the whole.

Let's *play a larger game* and evolve the very source code of consciousness and culture together.

With mad love,

The Editors

LOVE OR DIE

LOCATING OURSELVES: ARTICULATING THE ESSENTIAL CONTEXT FOR THE ONE MOUNTAIN, MANY PATHS ORAL ESSAYS

SETTING OUR INTENTION

Intention setting is everything.

We're here—as da Vinci was with his cohort in the Renaissance—**to play a larger game, to participate in the evolution of love, which is to tell the new Story of Value rooted in First Principles and First Values.**

- Our intention is to recognize the critical historical juncture in which we find ourselves.
- Our intention is to take our seat at the table of history and to say, *we take responsibility for this.*
- Our intention is to participate as revolutionaries for the sake of the whole.

What we're here to do is revolution; revolution for the sake of the evolution of love.

It's a revolution for the sake of the trillions of unborn lives that will not manifest:

- The unborn loves
- The unborn creativity
- The unborn goodness
- The unborn truth
- The unborn beauty

All of it looks to us.

Not because we're engaged in grandiosity. Not at all!

- We're trembling before She.
- We're trembling with joy at the privilege.
- We're trembling with joy at the responsibility.
- We're trembling with joy at the Possibility of Possibility.
- We have to enact a new Story in this moment of time. Because it is only a new Story that can change the vector of history.

The most revolutionary act that we can do—the greatest moral imperative of this time—**is to articulate a new Story at this time between worlds and this time between stories.**

Story is not made up, as postmodernity suggests. **We all live in inescapable frameworks; our framework is the story we live in.** Right now, Reality lives according to win/lose metrics, a story that is generating existential risk. **We need to change that story.**

When we change that story, when we tell a new Story—not a made-up story, but a new Story of Value, rooted in First Principles and First Values—**then it all changes.**

We need to participate in the evolution of the source code of consciousness and culture, which is the evolution of love.

It's the most important, exciting, evolutionary, revolutionary act that we can do to alleviate suffering: to be lovers.

Like Rumi, the great poet of Sufism, we have to be "mad lovers," because it's the only sanity.

To be mad lovers is to see around the corner, to not be so obsessed with the details of the contractions of my life.

Let me see bigger.

Let me take complete care of myself in every possible way, let me completely attend to those in my circle of intimacy and influence, and then—*let me expand my circle.*

That's what we're here for.

- Our intention is to participate in the *LoveForce*, the *LoveIntelligence*, the *LoveBeauty*, the *LoveDesire* that literally animates Cosmos all the way up and all the way down.
- Our intention is to participate in the evolution of love.

[*In the next few pages we will cover some key concepts which are essential to locating ourselves and setting the context for all the One Mountain, Many Paths Oral Essays. —Eds.*]

OVERVIEW: EROS IS NO LONGER A LUXURY—IT'S LOVE OR DIE

Eros is life.

The failure of Eros destroys life.

Our lack of Eros is poised to destroy the world.

All civilizations have fallen because the stories that they lived in were, in some sense, stories based on rivalrous conflict governed by win/lose metrics. Every civilization was weakened by interior polarization caused by the lack of a shared Story of Value.

We now have a global civilization, but we haven't created a shared Story of Value.

We haven't solved the generator functions that caused all civilizations to fall. Our global civilization has exponential technologies and extraction models depleting the Earth of resources that took billions of years to create, which is going to lead to a civilizational collapse.

Existential risk is risk to our very existence.

The choice is clear: love or die.

It's that simple.

Eros is no longer a luxury. It is an absolute necessity for the survival of the individual and the planet.

In the last half a century, modern psychology has documented an age-old truth: a fully nourished baby who is not held in loving arms will die.

So too, our world, both personal and global—even with all the resources of intelligence and technology at our disposal—will die without being held in love, in the embrace of Eros.

We must embrace a personal path of love and a global politics of love.

Not ordinary love. Not love which is "mere human sentiment," but Eros, or what we sometimes call Outrageous Love, which is the heart of existence itself.

We live in a world of outrageous pain.

The only response is Outrageous Love.

WHAT IS EROS?

Eros is the experience of radical aliveness, moving towards, seeking, desiring ever-deeper contact and ever-greater wholeness.[4] Eros is the core fabric of Reality's being and the motivational architecture of Reality's becoming.

Eros is what animates the evolutionary impulse itself, from the very inception of Cosmos all the way to our very selves, who awaken to the realization that the evolutionary impulse throbs uniquely in each of us.

The realization of human awakening and transformation that lies at the core of the interior sciences is the invitation—or even the urgent and desperate demand—of a madly loving Cosmos animated by infinities of power and infinities of intimacy.

The demand—the desperate invitation, the plea, the tender and fierce command of Cosmos that lives inside every human being—is to awaken: to awaken to our true nature as unique incarnations of Eros and Ethos that are needed and desperately desired by All-That-Is. Said slightly differently: Reality is Eros. Or: God is Eros.

The failure of Eros destroys life. The collapse of Eros is always the hidden (or not so hidden) root cause for the collapse of ethics.

This is true both personally and collectively. We live in a moment of a worldwide and personal collapse of Eros. Our lack of Eros is poised to destroy

---

[4] We define Eros through what we refer to as the Eros equation (one of a series of what we call interior science equations):

Eros = Radical Aliveness x *Desiring (Growing + Seeking)* x *Deeper Contact* x *Greater Wholeness* x *Self Actualization/Self Transcendence (Creation [Destruction])*

There are good reasons for the formal language of the interior science equations in these writings, and the reader is invited to explore them on their own, in particular, in our work, David J. Temple, *First Principles and First Values: Forty-Two Propositions on CosmoErotic Humanism, the Meta-Crisis, and the World to Come* (World Philosophy and Religion, 2024).

the world. Humanity is currently experiencing what has come to be known as existential risk, a risk to our very existence, or what I will refer to as the Second Shock of Existence.

EXISTENTIAL RISK: THE SECOND SHOCK OF EXISTENCE

The first shock of existence is the death of the human being—the realization that we will die, which dawns in human consciousness at the beginning of history. We are not talking about the biological fact of death but the *existential* realization of death. Although the interior sciences disclose that death is a portal between two days (there is vast empirical,[5] philosophical,[6] and anthro-ontological evidence[7] for the continuity of consciousness[8]), death is also, in our own direct surface experience, a stark end. And that is obviously not a bug but a feature in the system.

---

5   We refer to evidence gathered by the most serious of researchers, beginning with Henry and Edith Sedgwick at Cambridge University and William James at Harvard University, and continuing in highly rigorous form for the last 150 years, as recapitulated by Whiteheadian scholar David Ray Griffin in multiple volumes. See also, for example, Dean Radin, *Real Magic: Unlocking Your Natural Psychic Abilities to Create Everyday Miracles* (Potter/TenSpeed/Harmony, 2018), *The Conscious Universe: The Scientific Truth of Psychic Phenomena* (HarperCollins, 2010), and other books. Or see the earlier classic by Frederic William Henry Myers, *Human Personality and Its Survival of Bodily Death* (Longmans, Green, 1907).

6   This requires a cogent analysis of materialism and dualism, and the introduction of the far more cogent third possibility which we have called "pan-interiority."

7   We discuss Anthro-Ontology in some depth in *First Principles and First Values*, and see also the fuller conversation in David J. Temple, *First Principles and First Values: Towards an Evolving Perennialism: Introducing the Anthro-Ontological Method*—both published by World Philosophy and Religion Press, in Conjunction with Integral Publishers. For now, we will simply define it as an "innate and clear interior gnosis directly available to the human being."

8   See Dr. Marc Gafni and Dr. Zachary Stein's essay in preparation, "Beyond Death: Anthro-Ontology, Philosophy, and Empiricism." This essay is slated to appear in the book *Towards a World Religion: Homo Amor Essays*. The essay is also the ground for a larger book by the same authors, *Twelve Portals to Life Beyond Death: Responding to the Second Shock of Existence,* in which we discuss three forms of material: the empirical, the philosophical, and the anthro-ontological, and show how each form discredits the notion of death as the end.

Our first-person experience is that death ends this life. It is not the *totality* of our experience if we go deeper inside, but it is obviously intended to be the central, potent, and painful dimension of every human life. Indeed, as Ernest Becker potently reminded us, the denial of death is at our peril.

All the stories and all the plotlines and all the threads of living end at that moment. Whatever happens beyond, we have an actual experience of ending. **Paradoxically, that ending, the experience of the finality of mortality, is what presses us into life.** From the implicit demand of the first shock of existence, human beings were activated and pressed into creative emergence, and what emerged was all of human culture, both interior and exterior.

The second shock of existence is the realization of the potential death of all humanity. After all the stages of human history—matter, life, and mind in all of their stages of evolutionary unfolding—we have come to this place in the evolution of humanity, in which the gap between our exponentially expanding exterior technologies and our stalled (or even regressing) interior technologies of value has created dire catastrophic and existential risks.

This gap generates extraction models and exponential growth curves, rivalrous conflicts based on win/lose metrics, tragedies of the commons, and multipolar traps, in which everyone has to keep producing to the nth degree, including weaponized exponential threats to our very existence because we are afraid that the other parties are going to do it and not be transparent—hide it from us and then dominate us.

GENERATOR FUNCTIONS FOR EXISTENTIAL RISK

Let's outline clearly the main *generator functions for existential risk*.

Rivalrous conflicts governed by zero-sum, win/lose metrics. Rivalrous conflicts generate extraction models at the core of the economic system and exponential growth curves. Both of these drive and are driven by a contrived system of artificially manufactured desires and needs, delivered into culture by ever more precise forms of micro-targeting to individuals and groups through the ever more immersive environment of the internet.

Next, rivalrous conflicts and exponential growth curves animated by win/lose metrics generate **complicated, fragile world systems** highly vulnerable to myriad forms of collapse. Fragile local systems are made exponentially more fragile on a global level by our inability to meet global challenges with social, legal, political, economic, and ethical infrastructures that remain largely local.

All of this is a direct result of the failure to develop more adequate interior technologies that would be sufficiently compelling to displace "rivalrous conflict governed by win/lose metrics" as the motivational architecture for the human life world.

This failure has led to the conditions that will cause the implosion of systems that are already and quite literally on the brink of collapsing themselves. That's what we mean by the *second shock of existence*.

To recapitulate: the second shock of existence is not the death of the human being, but the potential death of humanity.

It is the *Death Star* moment of our species.

THE DECONSTRUCTION OF INTRINSIC VALUE

We stand in this moment poised between utopia and dystopia, at a time between worlds and a time between stories. We need a new Story of Value, eternal yet evolving, rooted in First Principles and First Values, which would become a universal grammar of value and a context for our diversity.

This is exactly what the Renaissance was. It was a time between worlds and a time between stories. In the Renaissance, we had recently been challenged by the Black Death, a pandemic that swept across Europe. The

Black Death destroyed between a third to half of Europe and a huge part of Asia. People died horrifically, brutally, in the streets. They had no idea how to meet this challenge, and so, in response to the Black Death, da Vinci and Ficino and their cohorts understood that they had to tell a new Story of Value.

That story was the story of modernity. Did they get it right?

- They got part of it right, which birthed, to use Jürgen Habermas' phrase, "the dignities of modernity," such as new ways of gathering information and universal human rights.
- But they also deconstructed the source of Value. They lost the basis for the Good, the True, and the Beautiful.

The basis used to be divine revelation: *God told us*. But this claim was owned by religion, and every religion began to overreach and over-claim. The revelation was thus often mediated through cultural categories and wasn't fully accurate.

Modernity threw out revelation, but was unable to establish a new basis for value.

Value was just assumed to be real. As it says in the founding document of the American Revolution: *We hold these truths to be self-evident*—that is, *we don't really have a basis for value; we just take it as a given.*

In other words, modernity took out a loan of social capital from the traditional world. The source of value was never worked out.

And then, gradually, value began to collapse.

- The Universe Story began to collapse.
- The belief that the Good, the True, and the Beautiful are real began to collapse.
- The belief that Love is real began to collapse.

As Bertrand Russell is reported to have said, "I cannot see how to refute the arguments for the subjectivity of ethical values, but I find myself incapable of believing that all that is wrong with wanton cruelty is that I do not like it."

What do you do if you grew up in a world in which value is not real? A world without a source of value, without a Universe Story, without a story of human identity, without a story of desire, without a narrative of power?

In the words of W.B. Yeats, *the center does not hold.*

- You have a collapse at the very center of society, because you no longer have Eros.
- You no longer have a Reality in which value is real, and so you have this lingering sense of emptiness.
- You have a complete collapse at the very center.
- We become *the hollow men and the stuffed men*, gesture without form.

And that's the source of our current existential risk.

THE DEEPER ROOT CAUSE OF THE META-CRISIS: A GLOBAL INTIMACY DISORDER

Above, I have outlined the major generator functions of existential risk. But there is a deeper cause for the existential risk that lurks underneath the rivalrous conflict governed by win/lose metrics and the fragile systems they engender.

And we cannot take the Death Star down without discerning and addressing this. We have already alluded to this root cause above, but at this point we need to make it more explicit so that, from this context, the adequate root response will become clear.

Modernity threw out the revelation, but was unable to establish a new basis for value.

This ostensibly surprising statement can be understood in a few simple steps:

1. All of the catastrophic and existential risk challenges we face are global: from climate change to artificial intelligence, pandemics, systems collapse, and exponential arms races.
2. Every global challenge self-evidently requires a global solution.
3. Global solutions can only be implemented with global co-ordination.
4. Global co-ordination is impossible without global coherence.
5. Global coherence is only possible if there is a global resonance between the parts.
6. Global resonance is only possible if we have global intimacy.

ONLY A SHARED STORY OF VALUE CAN GENERATE GLOBAL INTIMACY

Global intimacy—just like intimacy in a couple—is only possible when there is a shared story.

Not just a shared history, but a shared Story of Value.

- It is only a shared global story that can generate a new emergent quality of intimacy: global intimacy.
- A shared Story of Value must be rooted in shared ordinating values, or what we have called evolving First Values and First Principles.
- Intimacy requires a shared grammar of value as a matrix for a shared Story of Value.

The global intimacy disorder is the root cause for existential risk. The global intimacy disorder underlies the core generator functions for existential risk.

The global intimacy disorder is rooted in the failure to experience ourselves in a field of shared intrinsic value. This failure derives from the deconstruction of value.

Indeed, it is wholly accurate to say that **the root cause of the two generator functions of existential risk is the failed story of intrinsic value, or what we might also call the breakdown of Eros.**

1. The first generator function is **the success story.** Our modern success story is rivalrous conflict governed by win/lose metrics, which violates all the terms of the Intimacy Equation: there is no shared identity and no mutuality of recognition, feeling, value or purpose, and instead of *relative* otherness, there is *alienated* otherness. Such a story generates complicated fragile systems with no allurement or intimacy between the parts, systems which optimize for efficiency (as an expression of win/lose metrics) and not for resiliency and life.
2. The second generator function is **the deconstruction of intrinsic value** itself. The deconstruction of value is the sense that human value does not participate in the intrinsic value of the Real, for the Real is dogmatically declared to have no intrinsic value. Thus, there is no shared identity between the interior of the human being and Reality. There is no common participation in a field of shared intrinsic value. Instead of being intimate with value, we are alienated from value. And only intrinsic value can arouse will: political, moral, and social will.

To sum up, without a shared grammar of value there is no global intimacy, and therefore no global coherence, and no global coordination in response to catastrophic and existential risk, which means, put simply, there will be, quite literally, no future.

HEALING THE GLOBAL INTIMACY DISORDER REQUIRES THE EVOLUTION OF INTIMACY

But we are not hopeless. On the contrary, we are filled with great hope. Hope is a memory of the future. That memory of the future *is* the direct hit that takes down the Death Star, the culture of death. **The direct hit must be**—as it has always been in history—**the emergence of a new stage of evolution.**

Crisis is an evolutionary driver, and every crisis is, at its core, a crisis of intimacy: from the oxygen crisis of the single cells dying which generated multicellular life at the dawn of existence, to the existential risk in this very moment.[9]

The direct hit is therefore structurally self-evident: the evolution of intimacy itself.

What is intimacy, as a structure of Cosmos all the way down and all the way up the evolutionary chain? We engage this inquiry in depth in other writings, but for now we will simply adduce what we have called the "Intimacy Equation":

> Intimacy = *shared identity in the context of [relative] otherness* x *mutuality of recognition* x *mutuality of pathos* x *mutuality of value* x *mutuality of purpose*

Intimacy is about the capacity of parts to generate a *shared identity* while retaining their otherness, or distinct identity. This requires multiple mutualities, including recognition, pathos (or feeling), value, and purpose. The parts must recognize and feel each other, even as they share value and purpose. But all of this must lead to intimate union—and not pathological

---

[9] We demonstrate this principle in some depth in the multi-volume series, *The Universe: A Love Story* (forthcoming) (https://worldphilosophyandreligion.org/early-ontologies), *The Intimate Universe: Global Intimacy Disorder as Cause for Global Action Paralysis* (forthcoming), and in other writings of CosmoErotic Humanism.

fusion, where the distinct identity of the parts disappears—like subatomic particles that successfully become an atom, or two people who successfully become a couple.

THE DECONSTRUCTION OF VALUE IS THE DECONSTRUCTION OF INTIMACY

We have identified the global intimacy disorder as the root cause of existential risk. But the underlying ultimate failure of intimacy is the deconstruction of value itself.

The deconstruction of value means that human value does not participate in any sense of intrinsic value of the Real. This is not about individual *values,* but about *the Field of Value* that underlies all of them. **When the human being**—moved, often sincerely or even nobly, by myriad cultural, historical, and psychological confusions—**claims to have stepped out of the Field of Value, then intimacy itself is deconstructed.**

The deconstruction of value is the deconstruction of intimacy.

In the absence of a shared Story of Value, a story that is an authentic expression of Reality's Eros, a story rooted in *pseudo-Eros* takes center stage and becomes the generator function for existential risk. Our modern pseudo-Eros story is *rivalrous conflict governed by win/lose metrics.* Such a story catalyzes in its wake the second generator function of existential risk: *complicated fragile systems with no allurement or intimacy between the parts.* It is in that sense that we have argued that the first generator function for existential risk is the success story.

- The failure of intimacy is precisely the impotent experience that there is no shared identity between the interior of the human being and Reality. **There is no shared identity in the sense of any kind of common participation in a field of shared intrinsic value.**
- **But only a shared Story of Value can arouse the global will**

required to engage catastrophic and existential risk. For it is only global political, moral, and social will—and we can even say *erotic* will—that can generate the most Good, True and Beautiful world that we have always known is possible.

THE EVOLUTION OF LOVE IS THE TELLING OF A NEW STORY

Coupled with the Intimacy Equation is the scientifically grounded realization, in both the exterior and interior sciences, that Reality is a progressive deepening of intimacies, or, said slightly differently:

Reality is Evolution. Evolution is the evolution of intimacy.

- The evolution of intimacy requires—both personally and collectively—a deeper, more accurate discernment of the nature of our universe, ourselves, and our beloveds.
- This new discernment generates a new global Story of Value.
- The new global Story of Value generates an emergent, heretofore unseen global intimacy and heals the global intimacy disorder.

The new Story of Value is the direct hit that takes down the Death Star and replaces it with the hope that invokes the memory of our best future.

Global intimacy facilitates global coherence, which facilitates global coordination, which activates the possibility of our creative and effectively coordinated global responses to the global meta-crisis in its entirety and its specific expressions.

To solve Bertrand Russell's challenge—the apparent argument for the subjectivity of ethical values—**we have to reground value theory in eternal yet evolving First Principles and First Values, and articulate a new Story of Value.**

This is what we call CosmoErotic Humanism.

THE NEXT STEP IN CONSCIOUS EVOLUTION

CosmoErotic Humanism—together with other emergent strands—**needs to become the ground of a world religion as a context for our diversity**. We need religion, even as we need science, to articulate a shared global grammar of value.

As we said at the beginning, our choice is simple: love or die.

- To love means to participate in the evolution of love, which is the evolution of the human Story of Value.
- To love means to evolve and activate a new cultural enlightenment—rooted in a new narrative of identity, a new narrative of value, a new narrative of intimate communion, a new narrative of desire, a new narrative of power—all of which will birth new narratives of economics and politics.
- The evolution of love is the telling of a new Story.

The new Story that must be told is a love story, for in fact that is the deepest truth of Reality, rooted in the best exterior and interior sciences, that we have at this moment in time:

- Reality is not merely a fact. Reality is a story.
- Reality is not an ordinary story. Reality is a love story.
- Reality is not an ordinary love story. Reality is an Outrageous Love Story.

Story doesn't mean it's *made-up*.

It means doing the hard work of integrating the validated insights of the traditional world, the modern world, and the postmodern world.

This is the intention at the heart of telling the new Story of CosmoErotic Humanism.

ABOUT THIS VOLUME

We live in an Amorous Cosmos and the Amorous Cosmos lives in us. It's a Cosmos filled with desire and allurement.

Barbara Marx Hubbard and I were allured to each other in our shared desire to tell a new Story of Value. We both understood that the new story needs to have the depth and power to activate the emergence of a new human and new humanity, the next step in Conscious Evolution. We both understood that only such a Story of Value has the capacity to respond to existential risk—the risk to our very existence.

In other words, we understood that we live in a time between worlds, in a time between stories. And this time demands a new Story of Value, to take us to the next level which is the only way to usher in the "new world".

This book is a homage to the deep love and **whole mate relationship** between Barbara and me with all its beauty and challenges. It tells the story of how we deepened our intimacy through sometimes fierce contestation while modelling how to have evolutionary conversations as *Homo amor*.

Being *Homo amor* is to be kind and to be fierce yet filled with quivering tenderness. Being *Homo amor* is to apologize if you got it wrong and it is the willingness to give up being right. Homo amor is to fiercely stand for right, to know that the right is real, to move beyond polarization and to know that what unites is so much greater than what divides us, for we are all together in a Field of Value, before the field individuates into distinct values. We are value itself, before we are individual values.

ABOUT THIS VOLUME

To be ***whole mates*** is an evolution of conversation – in other words the capacity to hold an evolutionary conversation.

To be whole mates is to be covenanted and capacitated in evolutionary conversation.

To have an evolutionary conversation means *we want to impact each other from within the field of value, not to coerce each other but to synergize and transform together, evoking a new whole that is birthed in the depth of our encounter.* To have an evolutionary conversation is to love each other madly, to hold together a shared passion for truth goodness and beauty that is greater than our surface craving to be right. We give up being right for the sake of our shared higher passion.

To have an evolutionary conversation is to be capacitated to hold the fullness of contradiction, and not have it de-generate to polarization, but instead re-generate toward the mutually fructifying synergistic emergence of a new whole, a new story, a new paradox.

To have an evolutionary conversation is to step forward and to sometimes step back but to never turn away.

In these pages we honor and celebrate Barbara Marx Hubbard for her exceptional will and commitment to *not get older, but to get newer* every day. We testify that for Barbara this meant that she never stopped evolving, never froze her own development, never ossified into a contracted hardness. Barbara was heroically reaching for new depths of transformation until her very last days.

Barbara was one of the rare thinkers with that kind of courage, with that kind of intellectual integrity who fiercely examined her own positions, evolved them, regretted, and when confronted with genuine new information and insight, evolved her position in the most fundamental ways.

The reader is invited to witness parts of the evolutionary journey of Barbara and me joining genius in multiple modes.

We evolved together the understanding of Conscious Evolution. Picking up from the articulation of Barbara's Wheel of Co-Creation 1.0 (a visual schematic model which focused on connecting the leading-edge innovations in each of the sectors of the Wheel) we articulated the *Wheel of Co-Creation 2.0*. In Wheel 2.0 my core realizations of ErosValue and its expression as Desire being at the core of all of Reality are synergized with the original schema, with ErosValue and its Desire being understood as expression of the driving evolutionary impulse at the center of the wheel.

At the same time, I fiercely challenged Barbara's initial techno-optimism, with some of its potential shadow expressions. I pointed emphatically to the great danger of evolutionary spirituality leaning towards totalizing transhumanist solutions where the irreducibly unique value and dignity of human personhood was forgotten with unspeakably horrific results. Barbara and I aligned in the declaration that if transhumanist ideas were divorced from a shared Story of inherent Value, rooted in First Principles and First Values, then human beings faced existential risk, either in terms of extinction—the death of humanity—, or in terms of the death of *our* humanity; for example, in a world in which Artificial Intelligence coupled with reductive materialist assumption about the meaninglessness of humanity and therefore the utter fiction of human rights made human beings irrelevant to economics and politics. In such a world transhumanism merged with certain kinds of secularized Buddhism could easily become the ground for a worldwide totalitarianism and the death of *our* humanity. Indeed, in alliances between Jack Kornfield of Spirit Rock Meditation Center and Sam Altman of Open AI, and the shared rhetoric they espouse, we see more than just glimmers of these kinds of potential directions.

CosmoErotic humanism as unpacked in its major writings, demonstrates that moral will can only genuinely be aroused from the direct experience that value is not merely a fiction, but instead is the ultimate reality, the primordial ground in which all else arises. It is only such ground that can disclose the irreducible dignity of the personal, which is the only matrix in which human rights can survive the onslaughts of power history in all of its degraded forms.

CosmoErotic humanism declares that we can never *explain away* human suffering, through fundamentalist, New Age or scientistic attempts to rationalize or trivialize its existence. We cannot answer the theological question of suffering. But our incapacity to answer the question does not liberate us from the joy and responsibility of response. We must *respond* to human suffering with a new Story of Value which becomes the context for global intimacy, coherence and coordination. Indeed, it is only new Story of Value – the story of the intimate universe, that gives credence to our great protest against any and all forms of suffering. The *why do you allow suffering* only makes sense in an intimate world where there is a "YOU" an "I" and a "Thou", a *second person* who cares infinitely and intimately, where there is an Infinite Intimate, to whom the great crying out, the great protest is directed.

- We live in a world of outrageous pain; the only response to outrageous pain is Outrageous Love.
- We live in a world of outrageous beauty; the only response to outrageous beauty is Outrageous Love.

It is only Outrageous Love, which is the ground that gives permission, nay, which demands infuriated protests against outrageous pain. Ivan's speech to his brother Alyosha, in Dostoyevsky's 'The Brothers Karamazov', where he wants nothing to do with a God who allows boys to be ripped apart in pain by cruel generals and their dogs, is a model of just such a sacred protest. But for Ivan faith means the absence of protest and hence his outrage and protest necessarily cancel his faith. A deeper realization however would be that his protest itself is the mark of Outrageous Love and is the only possible response to the witnessing of outrageous pain.

This and more was the quality of discourse between us, a conversation which brought us into ever deeper whole mate alignment.

THE NEXT STEP IN CONSCIOUS EVOLUTION

With celebrating Barabara both on her birthday and on her day of passing into the next world, the lineages remind us that one's birthday and the day of death are of the same quality. In Aramaic they are called by a name that indicates both being born and passing. We have to know that death is not the end of the story. Every death is a night between two days, the darkness before the next birth.

The reader is invited to enter through 8 different doors to experience the anthro-ontological truth of the continuity of consciousness; yet to realize that at the same time death is also ultimately real. Experiencing the reality of death, presses us into life, to be fully here, fully committed, to be the change, to be living in the world that is already perfected. It is the reality of death that births us into the realization of the continuity of our lives—the unique current of ErosValue which is the quality of our unique intimacies.

The promise will be kept: to keep this movement of ecstatically birthing ever deeper Evolutionary Love, that Barabara and I initiated together, ever evolving. We must always come back, again and again to the core truth of realization: Reality is an Outrageous Love Story. And your story, each of our stories, are a unique chapter and verse in the larger unique story.

This knowing is the ultimate dignity of every human life. This is the only gnosis that can save our soul from shattering and our heart from breaking down and never recovering their pulse.

Volume 16

These oral essays are edited talks delivered by Marc Gafni and Barbara Marx Hubbard between December 2020 and April 2024.

CHAPTER ONE

CELEBRATING BARBARA MARX HUBBARD: THE PROMISE WILL BE KEPT

Episode 219 — December 20, 2020

CELEBRATING BARBARA'S 91ST BIRTHDAY

We are right before Christmas. It's 2020. New Year's a few days away. We'll hold the suffering of the world; we'll be in joy and in radical celebration.

We're beginning that celebration this week with a birthday party. I can't tell you how insanely delighted I am to be, on this day, celebrating my beloved evolutionary partner's, Barbara Marx Hubbard's, birthday. Barbara, your birthday is on the 22nd of December (2020), your 91st birthday.

I remember your 89th year so well. We were sure that we had at least five more years. You were healthy and vibrant and alive and filled, overflowing, with the ideas that we still had to realize in the world. Then, suddenly, you were sick. We were about to do a service on Sunday morning. I called you. You were okay the night before. We had talked the night before, we had prepared the service. We were laughing, you were delighted, about to get out of the hospital. During the night, a very hard moment, I called the hospital in the morning. We were actually right before

church, church was even starting, and I was calling you. You got on the phone. You said, "Marc." You were so excited, we were so excited, and it was the last word you spoke.

They took you downstairs. The second that our Evolutionary Church was over—I was then in California—I jumped on a plane. Sally Kempton drove me to the plane. I thought I'd get there, and you'd be awake. I was going to surprise you. *Wow!* I slept in your room on the couch that first night. Then your son came, and he took that place on the couch and I found another chair to sleep on. We were there for a few days together and you went to the next world. Oh my God. Today's your birthday and on your birthday, we do two things.

First, **we celebrate you.** Your birthday's the day on which Goddess decided she could not do it without Barbara Marx Hubbard, so we celebrate you on your birthday. You realize *Goddess decided She can't do it without me.*

Two, **on your birthday we also ask forgiveness.** It's a time of grace and so *I ask forgiveness, Barbara, for all the ways in which I couldn't show up as fully as you wanted me to do.* We spoke or communicated four, five times a day and yet still the fullness of what we wanted to manifest didn't quite happen. You made me promise before you passed and I said to you, "Yes, the promise will be kept."

The promise will be kept in this movement that all of us began together—Barbara, that you and I had the delight to initiate—of evolutionary love, this revolution, this moment in which we realize that in this time between stories and time between worlds we're going to tell the new story. The new story's not going to be fanciful conjecture. It's going to be the best integration of the validated truths of every major period of history—premodern, traditional, modern and postmodern—integrated together.

We came together to weave two dimensions of the new story.

One, which I'd written about, but it was your life focus: **Conscious Evolution**, and your beautiful book by that name. The second: **The Universe: A Love story** and **Unique Self Symphony**, the **Intimate Universe**, which were the *foci* of my life. And we said,

"Let's bring them together. Let's join genius,"—your word. "Let's actually birth together new mimetic structures. Let's birth together the new story in which we realize the realization of Unique Self and the realization that we're part of a Unique Self Symphony and the realization that we are actually *Homo amor*."

We created that word together. You used to talk about *Homo universalis*, and I started talking about *Homo amor*. For a while, we called it *Homo amor universalis*, but we decided that we just needed to merge *universalis* into *amor*. We wanted *amor* because *amor* is Love and *amor* is the Evolutionary Love story. You asked me and Ervin Laszlo to work on a book together with you about Evolutionary Love, and we have done that.

Oh my God. What's the basic knowing that you and I shared with each other every day?

- Reality's not merely a fact; Reality's a story.
- Reality's not an ordinary story; Reality's a Love story.
- Reality's not an ordinary Love story; Reality's an Evolutionary Love story, Reality's an Outrageous Love story.
- And your love story, our individual love stories, are chapter and verse in the Love story of the Universe.

We live in—and I want to share this word with everyone that Barbara, myself, and Howard Bloom created together—an "Amorous Cosmos." *Amor!*

We live in an Amorous Cosmos. It's a Cosmos filled with desire and allurement.

WE'RE IN CELEBRATION, AND IN OUR CELEBRATION IS ALL OF THE PAIN AND ALL OF THE JOY

Friends, love is in the details, so first off, I'm wearing a jacket today. I'm wearing a jacket because I wanted to get dressed up, Barbara, for your birthday party, mad celebration. This morning, we were thinking—and Kristina Kincaid asked— "What was Barbara's favorite song?" Of course, Barbara, what did I say? The song that you had talked to me about, that we would often start our own Holy of Holies[1] study with, that we would send back and forth to each other, *Chariots of Fire*. Barbara, today we're going to listen to *Chariots of Fire*.

We're going to hear you talk about what you and I created together—we wrote it on a napkin in Portland just a few weeks before you passed—**the Wheel of Co-Creation 2.0, which was the penultimate expression of our integrated memes.**

- We are in celebration.
- We are in celebration of Reality.
- We are in celebration of Christmas to come, New Year's to come.
- We are in celebration of the enormous dignity of humanity that's been able to find a vaccine within 10 months of the outbreak of a plague—unheard of in human history.

And, in our celebrations, we feel all the pain of the world:

It's the 1,500,000 people who've passed, across the globe, during the Covid pandemic in 2020. It's the 300,000 people who've passed in America. It's the people all over Europe and Asia.

> *In our celebration is all of the pain and all of the joy.*

---

[1] *Holy of Holies* is what Dr. Marc Gafni calls private study conversations

We breathe with everyone who's on a ventilator [in late 2020, during the Covid pandemic].

We're with every single family, and many of them are families who are in desperate financial situations.

We pour our energy and our resource every place and everywhere we can.

Our key focus is, that we have to change the whole thing. We have to—like da Vinci and Marsilio Ficino did—tell a new story, a shared, universal grammar of value, as a context for our diversity, that raises all boats.

So, oh my God, friends, let's celebrate today like we've never celebrated before.

Let's look at our first clip, from the movie's *Chariots of Fire*, opening scene.

[Clip: *Chariots of Fire*, Titles scene]

WE NEED LINE AND CIRCLE QUALITIES AT HIGHER LEVELS OF CONSCIOUSNESS

I want to just share one thing about Barbara, which is just incredibly beautiful. One of the reasons that Barbara loved this music, and we loved it together, is because it celebrated the masculine. It's one of the things that was so special about Barbara, one of many things, that she celebrated the masculine in an era in which—and Barbara and I talked about it often—the masculine was being demonized. In part the masculine was being critiqued and called to a higher evolution, which is important; but there was also and is also a fundamental demonization of the masculine in the space.

Just as in the black/white conversation all around the world, there's this demonization of whiteness. There's this identity politics in which large groups of people are, as a class, held to be fundamentally flawed.

Barbara said *no* to that in a huge, gorgeous way. Barbara held in her witness a celebration of the masculine. Her beautiful husbands, whom she would talk about a lot—Earl, her first husband; Sidney, her second husband; Jonas Salk, a great love of her life, who was a deep and important part of her life. As Barbara and I worked together as evolutionary partners and whole mates, she held this celebration of the masculine.

As we watch these clips, let's have a moment where we celebrate the masculine. It's so deep and it's so profound.

I want to just add one word, so we get this really clear.

We always celebrate the feminine and we always celebrate the masculine, but here's the key. We don't need more masculine values. We don't need more feminine values. It's a huge mistake.

My friend Raj Sisodia, who wrote the book *Conscious Capitalism* with John Mackey, wrote me a draft of one of his new books a few years ago and it was all about the celebration, "We need more feminine values." I wrote him back, *Raj, no!*

We don't need more feminine values or more masculine values. We need more feminine and masculine values at higher levels of consciousness.

Masculine and feminine doesn't mean men and women.

Masculine and feminine are what we call the line and circle that live in each one of us.

We're all masculine and feminine in a larger, unique integration, what we call unique gender.

We've got to move beyond He and She and own the full line and full circle quality—the full masculine and feminine—that lives in each of us.

We talk about line qualities as this quality of breaking through, this quality of radical steadiness, this directionality, this sense of thrusting forward, this purpose driven, that's one dimension.

Then we talk about the feminine or the circle qualities such as the quality of holding and nurturing and qualities of radiance.

We don't just need *more* of either of those qualities. For example, let's say we have more feminine values at *ethnocentric consciousness*: You've got all sorts of Nazi mothers or Ku Klux Klan mothers nurturing their kids and raising them to run—in the case of Nazis—concentration camps. It's a big deal, but they're nurturing and they're loving their kids and they're being radiant and beautiful. No! That's not what we need.

We want feminine values not at egocentric and ethnocentric consciousness.

We want feminine values at worldcentric and cosmocentric consciousness in which we have a felt sense of love, care and concern for every human being and for the whole planet.

We want masculine values of purpose-driven and of thrusting-forward and of directionality and of sharp distinctions—not at an egocentric or ethnocentric level of consciousness, which causes war, devastation and destruction that's unbelievable, because it becomes an us/them and win/lose metrics. *No!* That's not what we need.

We want to move from ego self to Unique Self in which men are at a worldcentric consciousness and cosmocentric consciousness, in which the masculine is breaking through, playing its part as an instrument in a larger Unique Self Symphony in which all of that masculine energy goes into radical uniqueness.

---

*That masculine energy lives in all of us,
and that feminine energy lives in all of us.*

Barbara loved the song because she felt the evolutionary impulse in it. The evolutionary impulse doesn't have the face of God or the face of Goddess. It is: God/Goddess is one. It's not a man or a woman. It's masculine and feminine as one. It's beyond He and She.

We're in mad celebration of Barbara, who was profoundly masculine—profoundly driven, profoundly thrusting forward all the time—and yet at the same time nurturing and nourishing and all about celebration.

In the last few weeks of her life, she was with us in Portland and every afternoon, at about four or five o'clock Barbara would go get a couple of bottles of wine and she'd say, "It's time for cocktails." I'd keep working, and the women would go into the living room, the great feminine, and they would drink those bottles, and they would celebrate every single day for the couple of weeks we were together. Celebration!

We've got a great code today. It's a code that is going to be celebrated by Barbara in her talk. We're going to crescendo today with a gorgeous (recorded) talk by Barbara on the Wheel of Co-Creation 2.0[2].

EVOLUTIONARY LOVE CODE: YOU ARE A UNIQUE SET OF ALLUREMENTS

> Reality is Eros. Reality is Desire, Allurement, and Intimacy—the three faces of Eros.
>
> You are a unique configuration of Eros, Desire, Intimacy, and Allurement. Your deepest heart's desire is the desire of evolution awakening in you, as you, and through you.
>
> You are a unique set of allurements. Your allurement and desire perfectly match the deepest needs in your unique circle of Eros, Intimacy, and influence. In meeting those unique needs, uniquely addressed by you, you meet your own deepest need and fulfill your deepest heart's desire.

---

[2] During these memorial, celebrational episodes we would play recorded sermons of Barbara to keep her legacy alive

SUCCESS 1.0, SUCCESS 2.0, SUCCESS 3.0

We're going to look at the Wheel of Co-Creation 2.0. I'm going to first briefly introduce it and set it up. The Wheel of Co-Creation 2.0 is probably the most potent visual image of the new story that needs to serve as the basis of a global ethos for a global civilization, as a context for our diversity.

***add image Wheel of Co-Creation 2.0

We're in a moment of failed coherence. **Coherence means it all fits together: there's a larger, shared identity between the parts that create a new whole.** It's not a win/lose metrics governed by rivalrous conflict, which itself is the core root source or the *generator function* of existential risk.

We, Barbara and I together, ran a program in 2014 called Success 3.0:

- In Success 1.0, you're obedient to God, you're successful.
- Success 2.0 is rivalrous conflict, governed by a win/lose metrics. My value is in my productive capacity. I'm a separate self individual. I've got to create and produce; and if I produce, I get rewarded, which is beautiful. There's enormous beauty to that motivational architecture; but at its core it created this notion of a failure of intrinsic value to the human being—number one. Number two, it created an uneven playing field; and number three, I am rewarded only if I produce certain structures, let's say a new app, for example. I'm not rewarded for producing value. I'm rewarded for producing something that will be gobbled up by the marketplace even if I appeal to the lowest common denominator of the marketplace. This is what's been created, not by capitalism, but by the shadows of capitalism.

Barbara and I, we did this together with John Mackey and Jack Canfield and Ben Jealous; and Tony Hsieh was with us—who has passed away and blessing to Tony Hsieh. And there was Tom Chi, Arianna Huffington and so many fabulous people. We did this incredible gathering to envision this new possibility, this new vision of success. We called it Success 3.0.

- Success 3.0 is the new story which is the realization of this new vision of identity, this vision of *Homo amor,* the fulfilment of *Homo sapiens,* in which I'm a Unique Self giving my unique gift. My Unique Self is the unique configuration of desire and Eros that is me.

Out of that comes the Wheel of Co-Creation 2.0 that we'll look at together and we'll hear Barbara talking about, friends; but before we do that, we're going to pray.

PRAYER AFFIRMS THE PERSONHOOD OF COSMOS

First, we're going to go directly into prayer now. When we pray—I want to just hold this really tightly with you—we're not leaving science behind. We're not leaving the deepest movement of the human mind and heart. Prayer's an affirmation of a First Principle and First Value of the personhood of Cosmos. I want to get that sentence again.

Prayer is not a dogma; prayer is a realization. Prayer is an affirmation of the First Value and First Principle of the personhood of Cosmos.

There are three primordial perspectives:
It/He/She/They/Them/third person—the energy that moves through Cosmos, the laws of physics, all of that, billions of light years, spacetime curvature. The four forces. Those are the third-person forces.
There's first person, the experience of "I." That's a second primary First Principle and First Value of Cosmos.
And then there's second person, the great Thou, the great Other. Personhood. Relationship. The personhood of Cosmos, Divinity, God. *The*

god you don't believe in doesn't exist. But one of the faces of Spirit is the personhood of Cosmos, which is not just the intimacy that lives between You and I, but it's the Infinity of Intimacy in which our personal intimacy participates.

So, we turn to God.

Barbara and I, we'd pray together in Evolutionary Church every week, and we would text each other as the song *Hallelujah* played. We'd sing it together and around the world. So, Leonard Cohen, be with us to celebrate Barbara Marx Hubbard's birthday, the *holy and the broken Hallelujah*. Oh my God. Take us inside, Leonard Cohen. Let's pray.

[Music: *Hallelujah* by Leonard Cohen]

Oh my God. Friends, let's lift our prayers to the sky. Let's lift it like we've never lifted it before. Our love is lifting us higher and we are impressing our love on the lips of the Divine as we stand as evolution.

We are the personal face of evolution itself. We are Unique Self and Evolutionary Unique Self.[3]

THE WHEEL OF CO-CREATION 1.0

Barbara created the original Wheel of Co-Creation 1.0, and at the core of the Wheel of Co-Creation 1.0 are the sectors of the Wheel. On the outermost rung of the Wheel, you'll find health, infrastructure, justice, media, relationships, sciences, spirituality, arts, economics, etcetera. So there are 12 different sectors of the Wheel. This is a critical idea that Barbara really

---

3 For more information on Evolutionary Unique Self and all of the "five selves" please see the essay "Integrating the Two Models of Self" (https://worldphilosophyreligion.substack.com/p/integrating-the-two-models-of-self), as well as the book, Awakening Your Unique Self.

championed gorgeously for fifty years. The core of this is what Barbara called *social synergy:* let's connect what is working worldwide. Take a look at the top of the Wheel where it says, "Social synergy." So, the outer rung of the Wheel is the sectors of the Wheel and the idea is that we want to take the leading-edge creations, the leading-edge innovations, in each of the sectors of the Wheel and connect them to each other, because no sector of society lives by itself.

Everything is inter-included and if we create social synergy between the leading edge of what's already working and connect all of those dimensions worldwide, we'll realize that a lot of the new story is already in play, it's already being enacted on the fringes, on the periphery. We've got to take those periphery enactments which are the leading edge and link them together. That's the core of the Wheel of Co-Creation 1.0.

THE WHEEL OF CO-CREATION 2.0

What we've done is in the Wheel of Co-Creation 2.0, we've got an entirely next-step-world. **At the center of the Wheel 2.0, together with Barbara, we placed *desire*.** That's really important. That's only in the Wheel 2.0.[4]

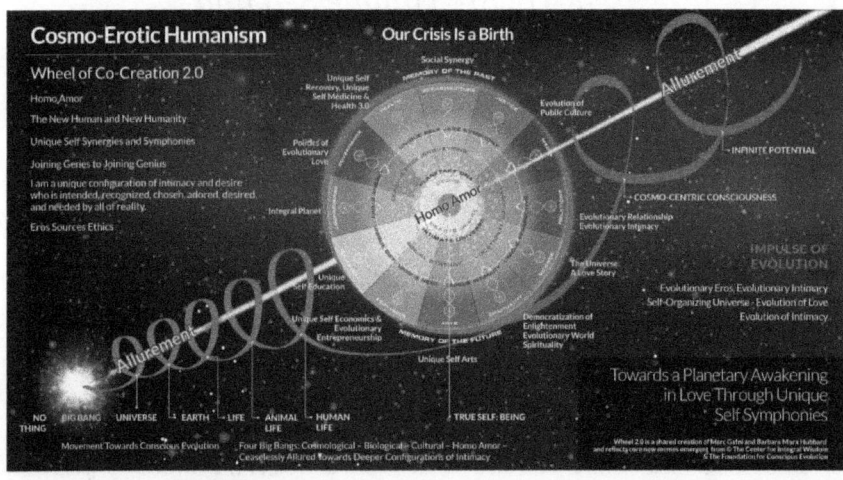

---

4 Image of the Wheel of Co-Creation 2.0: https://centerforintegralwisdom.org/wp-content/uploads/2019/05/Wheel-of-Creation-FEB-2019-V1-01-1024x545.jpg

Desire is the center of the Wheel 2.0 because there's a realization that Reality is desire.

That's the core of our code this week. Reality is appetite. Alford North Whitehead talked about the "appetition" of Cosmos and he used the word "appetition" because he was in Cambridge and an Englishman in the 1920s, but by "appetition" he means desire.

- Reality desires Value.
- Reality generates Value.
- Reality desires to generate ever more Value.

That desire is the desire for the Good, the True, the Beautiful.

It's the desire for ever more uniqueness.

It's the desire for ever more love.

It's the desire for ever more wholeness.

It's the desire for ever more creativity.

At the core it's not tepid, it's not flaccid, it's not neutral: It's desire!

Now, that desire lives in us. If you look at the center of the Wheel, right across from desire you have "heart's desire" and that's your deepest heart's desire. Desire and deepest heart's desire, that is the planetary DNA of the Intimate Universe.

1. Deepest heart's desire is the *planetary DNA* of the Intimate Universe. That's critical.
2. Now, that deepest heart's desire generates *vocational arousal*— that's the next circle. Vocational arousal generates leading-edge innovations. And when we link the leading-edge innovations, we get social synergy.

3. Then you go to the next circle in the Wheel. That circle with the purple text is the core of *Unique Self*, and it says "your unique story," and "your unique gift" and "your unique presence," "your unique quality of intimacy," and those dimensions of uniqueness come together to form Unique Self Symphony.

That's critical.

When I awaken, I awaken from separate self, but not just to True Self. As the enlightenment traditions used to teach, True Self means *I'm one with everything, I'm part of the seamless coat of consciousness.* Yes, that's true, that is the change that changes everything, but it's only the first step. The next step is that I awaken from True Self to Unique Self, and I realize that every Unique Self sees through a unique set of eyes.

Every Unique Self has a unique perspective and participates in a unique quality of intimacy. My unique quality of intimacy, my unique perspective, creates my unique capacity to give my unique gift.

Together we come together in Unique Self Symphony and that Unique Self Symphony then animates the next dimension of the Wheel, which is the 12 sectors of Reality.

Wow! Then if you look around the next circle on the wheel, you've got:

- Unique Self recovery.
- Unique Self medicine.
- Politics of Evolutionary Love.
- Integral planet.
- Unique Self education.
- Unique Self arts.
- Democratization of enlightenment.
- Evolutionary World Spirituality.
- The Universe: A Love story.

All of these are the memes that we're working on at the Center for Integral Wisdom[5], and at the Foundation for Conscious Evolution, to try and develop this new story for a new humanity.

Let's just look at one more thing, and then Barbara will pick it up. Look at the top left where it says, "Wheel of Co-Creation 2.0." At the very center of the Wheel is *Homo amor*. *Homo amor* is at the very, very center of the Wheel. That's the new human and the new humanity. The new human and new humanity participate in (see left side of the image) Unique Self Synergies and Symphonies. We move from just joining genes to joining genius. We understand this new dimension of identity, that:

I'm a unique configuration of intimacy and desire who's intended, recognized, chosen, adored, desired and needed by all of Reality. That sense of Eros that lives uniquely in me animates my ethics.

All of that is the trajectory of Cosmos. Look at the Wheel, where it says *allurement*.

1. Cosmos begins with no-thing.
2. Cosmos is motivated, animated, by allurement; and allurement moves through (see bottom of image) the first Big Bang, then comes Universe, Earth, matter. Then life, followed by human life and consciousness. Those are the three Big Bangs.
3. At the very center of *Homo amor*, at the center of the Wheel, you've got that gold circle that says True Self being. The center of *Homo amor* is True Self, and **Homo amor is a unique expression of True Self.**
4. Finally, at the bottom right, we see, *Where's this moving?* Towards a Planetary Awakening in Love through Unique Self Symphonies.

With so much delight, I turn the word to you. Barbara Marx Hubbard.

---

5 Now called Center for World Philosophy and Religion, see https://worldphilosophyandreligion.org/

EVOLUTIONARY INTELLIGENCE EQUALS DESIRE

When we go up this enormous evolutionary story, billions of years, you can see that at the core of creation, **allurement is driving the entire system forward**, because what else would be doing it?

What is the system desiring? To go from single cell to multi-cell, to animal, to human. **There is a pattern that seems to be what nature desires: to get us here, to this moment.**

Nature desires to connect separate parts.

Nature desires to move through the billions of years of complexity motivated by no-thing at all, which is pure desire. We get to us without God entering into the process to do anything. That is to say, they used to think God just did it by hand. But God did *not* do this by hand, and it happened way before consciousness and way before scientists. As Brian Swimme says, *there were no scientists making up photosynthesis*. Photosynthesis is about the most complex invention that nature went through in that time and did it exquisitely.

So, first of all **we have to really honor the heart of desire**. We have to say not only is it amazingly brilliant, but let's just say *intelligent*, if you want to extend that word, a *gorgeously brilliant godlike brilliance* that could have gotten all those single cells to join together to make multi-cells.

If reality could invent photosynthesis by desire, well then, folks, what can *we* do with desire? If the Universe could create us with—I think the latest estimate is 52 trillion cells—let's think of that as an embodiment of desire. Who did that? We don't even know. I sometimes think of a thumb or an eye or an ear and I think of the enormity of intelligence needed to create that. **If we equate evolutionary intelligence with desire, we are elevating desire way beyond what its ordinary meaning.**

I think Marc is right in saying: Allurement is that what connects the connectivity of all these parts that are linking these very complex wholes.

Did somebody *tell* them all to organize? Did they *tell* the quarks to do this? Who told the quarks to get together? Who told the electrons?

So, in other words—I hadn't really thought of it until now—we get a glimpse of the enormity of desire and intelligence. Enormous! Then we realize that desire (through intelligence) starts making new whole systems that have never been seen before on Earth. As Brian Swimme said, there is no scientist he knows of who could have imagined how to create a single cell, create multi-cells, create photosynthesis.

Let's really access the heart of desire being intelligence, which is moving toward... what? Not toward dominance and control, because you know what? Billions of species are extinct. It's not all that successful at control. **Intelligence of no-thing attracts us to each other to create greater wholes that, together, are far more intelligent and desirous than the sum of their parts**. So, you might even say God is in favor of desire.

DEEPEST HEART'S DESIRE AND THE DNA OF AN EMERGING CULTURE

Let's start with Him or Her or It, let's start with Source.

Source is attracted to desire. Source sourced desire.

Think of all these species dropping out, billions and billions of them gone forever. But some ones kept going, and there are people who've analyzed how species survived and how species did not survive. But now we humans got up here and, of course, with the atomic bomb, we can destroy ourselves. I didn't go that whole way when I first thought of it, but now **I can see that**

this is Source coming through us as the impulse of creation. That, for me, is really a version of evolutionary meditation.

It's not going into the no-thing at all. It's going into incarnation of impulse as Divine.

Yes? The incarnation of the evolutionary impulse is the Divine impulse toward desire to join together, to create more life. You can't do it alone and you can't do it in an additive way by just getting together.

In other words:

- You have to yearn for each other.
- You have to have longing at the source of it.
- You have to have sexuality at the source of it.
- You have to have supra-sexuality at the source of it.

Nature has made desire to be at the source of creation. Now let's imagine the heart of the hub of the Wheel with this desire at the core for our meditative practices. What we're really getting in touch with is not simply *no-thing at all* but *every-thing that is,* because *no-thing at all* has co-created *every-thing that is*. Who and what and how is it happening now inside us? So, *no-thing at all* can be *every-thing that is,* in other words, it is incarnating the evolutionary impulse.

I would like to suggest that when we go out of meditation here around this. Marc has already talked about deepest heart's desire. I want to talk about our deepest *personal* heart's desire as what we have to cultivate at the core of the Wheel of Co-Creation.

I've been asking a lot of people, "What is your deepest heart's desire?" It's not easy to answer.

If you go deep down into your deepest heart's desire, do you know what you will find? The impulse of creation that is Divine. You find God. You find Source.

When I go into Source as the deepest heart's desire and longing in me, I find the impulse for creation that is yearning to join with others like this in order to fulfil what *is* my deepest heart's desire.

I keep going to the planetary awakening like I'm driven by an impulse until the time the connectivity on the planet is sufficiently great and we're all in the sectors of the wheel. It's what Marc calls the Planetary Awakening in Love through Unique Self Symphonies. I think that's why we came together. The point is:

> *In your deepest heart's desire resides the blueprint of your evolutionary potential.*

If you want to know what's *really* special about your creativity, that's not so easy to know. It's not so easy to know either your deepest heart's desire or your unique gift that *realizes* your deepest heart's desire that you want to express in such a way that other people want to join you.

We put at the *heart,* at the hub, of the Wheel of Co-Creation **people's deepest heart's desire revealing to them the uniqueness of their creativity.** We talk about the Unique Self, but the Unique Self ultimately has to be able to express your *Evolutionary* Unique Self, and I have found most people do not know! **But it's not that they don't have it. It's just that it hasn't been cultivated.**

What should be the structure of a society which is going to create through a Wheel of CoCreation with all these different sectors so that that's more obvious? We can go into social synergy, which we're not doing now, but here's an interesting thought:

The structure or planetary DNA of an emerging culture of humanity right now would be designed by a symphony of their deepest heart's desires. In other words, you catch a glimpse of it. Like, my deepest heart's desire, let's say, is a planetary awakening in love through a Unique Self Symphony with Conscious Evolution fully known in the world. I can really design a beautiful heart's desire here. But what would I put in planetary DNA about that? I have to do something about that.

> *I'm not just sitting there desiring something. I am going to take action.*

I'm here doing this and I'm doing that. So, **planetary DNA starts to be the early phase of a new culture**; because it's what people want to do! It's also what people want to do *from* their deepest heart's desire.

So, just in conclusion here, it is an awesome thought that out of no-thing at all, coming up through billions and billions of years of evolution, we have come to the moment where we're at the threshold of extinction. And at that moment our Conscious Evolution, that we would be able to offer to each other and then to a larger society and communities throughout the world, through our internet and other ways, **an opportunity for people to express their deepest heart's desire with the longing to join genius exactly where you need it to fulfil your heart's desire**. Let's do that!

I DON'T GROW OLDER, I GROW NEWER

Can you feel that? I'm so delighted to feel Barbara [through this recorded sermon of hers], and I'm also just heartbroken. I miss Barbara terribly. **She stood with the evolutionary impulse. We stood together with the evolutionary impulse** in this unflagging, unshakeable way. It doesn't mean—and I want to share this with everyone with tears in my eyes—that it **wasn't often hard for Barbara**. Often, she called me depressed and she'd say, "I'm depressed! And so many of my friends have died. And we haven't gotten there yet. "

And then she would *find* herself. She would go in and look for herself. She would practice. We would chant. She would journal. She would find herself and then, out of that finding of herself, she would come back recharged.

We all fall. We all contract.

To live filled with and animated by Outrageous Love doesn't mean that it's automatic. It doesn't mean that we're on some constant steroids. That is not what we mean at all. It means that:

> *We laugh out of one side of our mouth, and we cry out of the other side of our mouth.*

Barbara was completely committed every single day: "I want to evolve today. I want to grow today. I want to be more today than I was yesterday." That's what she meant when she said, echoing Abraham Kook, whose commentary on the *Song of Songs* says the exact same words:

"I don't grow older, I grow newer."

Wow! Friends, can you feel that with me? Oh my God. Friends, that's the feeling.

BARBARA RAN FOR EVOLUTION

We're about to watch a race. This is Barbara's favorite scene of *Chariots of Fire*. But imagine this not as a race but as a Unique Self Symphony.

In the old model it's rivalrous conflict. In the new model, every one of those young men who are racing—and it can be young men and young women and, thank God, women are in track now—but every one of those young people who are racing, they're not racing *against* each other.

They're running for the glory of Evolution.

THE NEXT STEP IN CONSCIOUS EVOLUTION

Let's see this and let's pray this together. This is our prayer. Barbara, your favorite scene. Happy birthday. Coming inside. All the way. Here we go.

[*Chariots of Fire, final scene*]

Oh my God, friends. Can you feel that?

Friends, Barbara ran for evolution. Barbara ran for She.

But as Barbara would tell you in this moment—you know what we're about to say—every one of us is Eric Liddell and Harold Abrahams, the runners in the movie. Each one of is are Unique Selves. Eric is a Scottish missionary running for the pleasure of God. Which he didn't even quite know yet is the pleasure of evolution. Harold Abrahams is an English Jew running to transcend prejudice, to transcend anti-Semitism and to live in a world where we're judged by the content of our character and not by the color of our skin.

Feel it. Feel the crowds going wild. Can you feel the crowd? Why are the crowds going wild? Because they can feel the spirit of evolution moving.

So, friends, Barbara, beloved, tears in my eyes, Barbara Marx Hubbard, you are running still in utter continuity of consciousness. We miss you madly and we're with you and we're going to continue. This is your home on this planet, this weekly gathering of *One Mountain, Many Paths*. This gathering every week is your home and we're going to continue to play clips of your teaching and to hear you and to be with you and to hold hands and, at this moment between stories, to make it all happen together.

Love you madly, Barbara.
Thank you so much.

Oh my God, happy birthday, Barbara. Happy birthday.

CHAPTER TWO

THE CONTINUITY OF CONSCIOUSNESS: DEATH IS NOT THE END OF THE STORY

Episode 234 — April 4, 2021

WE RESPOND TO THE FIRST AND SECOND SHOCKS OF EXISTENCE

We're here poised between utopia and dystopia. We're poised between a heaven that's unimaginable—the ability, the capacity to create a response to an immensity of suffering that has never before been possible in human history—and we're poised between unimaginable dystopia, destruction, and devastation.

In this moment poised between, we realize that we face catastrophic risk and existential risk, what we call here the "second shock of existence."

- The first shock? The realization that the individual human dies.
- The second shock, so much later, after all the stages of human history? The realization not of the death of the individual human being, but of the potential death of humanity.

On Easter—and this morning's the last day of Passover and it's the day of Easter—we look to both the first shock and the second shock together:

We respond to the first shock, which is the death of the human being. We speak the Dharma of resurrection, the Dharma of the interior science of the truth, of the deep fact of the continuity of consciousness.

At the very same moment, we speak to the second shock of existence—to the potential death of humanity—and we understand that **the only response to the death of humanity is the evolution of consciousness itself.**

*The evolution of consciousness itself is the realization that **I am evolution**.*

My deepest heart's desire is aligned, is an expression of the very desire of evolution itself.

My true freedom is to align with the evolutionary impulse and to feel the evolutionary impulse beating, throbbing, pulsing uniquely in me, as me, and through me—intending me, desiring me, choosing me, adoring me, loving me, needing me.

Knowing that *Reality needs my service* —**not as a metaphor, not as a trifling poetic flight of fancy, not as a conjecture, but as the very core of my identity**.

I'm not merely *Homo sapiens*. I'm not merely a separate self striving for status in win/lose metrics. I'm *Homo amor*, the new human.

The rising of Christ is the realization that I am utterly needed by All-That-Is.

I am evolution itself in person

Evolution awakens in me as Conscious Evolution. Conscious Evolution means I become awake to the truth that evolution lives in me, as me, and through me—and that it doesn't end when it's over.

DEATH IS NOT THE END OF THE STORY

It doesn't end with the death of humanity, and it doesn't end with the death of the individual human being, but there's a profound continuity of consciousness.

BARBARA IS WITH US IN THE CONTINUITY OF CONSCIOUSNESS

I've been thinking a lot in the last few weeks of my dear beloved wholemate, Barbara Marx Hubbard. Barbara and I together were madly delighted to cofound this space, this revolution, this global communion of pioneering souls. We spoke for 130, 140 weeks together, we were in this space of *One Mountain, Many Paths* together. Barbara's going to be speaking to us this morning.

One of the things that Barbara and I spoke about most often was the continuity of consciousness. We had some of our most profound conversations on Easter Saturdays and Easter Sundays. I want to ask you, *who among you can feel and know Barbara's continuity of consciousness with us in this moment, right here and right now?*

Barbara's with us, a thousand percent. I stand for that. I know that.

Barbara, welcome. You've never gone, and I miss you insanely and I'm so delighted and ecstatic to have you with us this morning, that you're going to be speaking. We were talking yesterday about how much we missed you, and you're with us. We're holding hands that way you used to come up next to me and you'd kind of crook your hand in mine in that way that we're walking elbow in elbow, and you'd talk about what the next project and what next iteration could be.

We realized that we need a center for the revolution.

But it's not just a revolution; it's a Renaissance, meaning it's a flowering of evolution; it's a flowering of new ideas. The core of this Renaissance, the core of what we need to do today in this time between worlds, in this time between stories, is to tell a new story.

But that new story's got to be *told*, it has to be located in local communities, in bottom-up, self-organizing systems.

We are such a local community. **But the local communities**—and this is the core to the new Renaissance—**need to become global**. We're *One Mountain, Many Paths,* and there's a thousand of us maybe at the core of the community as we've begun it in these last couple of years. As this local community, bound by bonds of Outrageous Love, we come together. We speak, every week, the new story. We articulate through the Evolutionary Love Codes new pieces, new dimensions, new chapters of the new story.

Then we need to take that new story—at the core of which is the planetary awakening in love through Unique Self Symphonies—and we need to invest, to download, to penetrate in the most wondrous way, to share that new story with the very nervous system of the planet.

The reason we have an internet is not for it to be commodified, not for *surveillance capitalism*, described so well by Shoshana Zuboff.

The reason we have an internet is to be able to share, evolve the new story with the planet itself, growing this revolution.

And that's who we are.

We're a revolution.

We're standing for the new story.

We're in the new Renaissance.

We're standing against existential risk.

And we understand that all the new technologies—all the techno solutions, all the new forms of ledgers and blockchains—it's all interesting, but none of it's going to take us home.

The only thing that's going to take us home is to do what da Vinci did, to gather together the strands, weave together a new fabric. **That new fabric is the new story, based on First Principles and First Values, which becomes the ground for a global ethos for a global civilization.**

Barbara, it's what I've lived my whole life for.

It's what you lived your whole life for.

It's what so many of us gathered here today have lived our whole lives for.

THE MOVEMENT TO RESURRECTION

We're going to talk today about death, but moving *beyond death*. Not the illusion of death, but the movement to resurrection.

Oh my God, what an intention! What a moment. What a glory. What an enormous pain in the world. There's so much pain in the world. There's such a gap between our "palace of imagination" and our "palace of reality."

To close that gap, we have to put one foot in front of the other, step at a time, and find each other—conversation by conversation, groundswell by groundswell, selforganizing relationship by selforganizing relationship.

We must be mad, Outrageous Lovers sharing the good news, building step by step, project by project, text by text, broadcast by broadcast—madly committed, radically present, fully alive.

Let that aliveness, and let that goodness, and let that truth, and let that beauty, like a mighty river, suffuse Reality.

Oh my God, it is so wondrous to be together. Barbara, I want to say it for the last time, welcome. Let's see if we can meet each other and just say, *Bar-*

bara, thank you. Thank you for being here with us today. All of the interior scientific and the *radical empirical data*, as William James would put it, tells us that **death is an illusion**. We're going to talk about that this morning.

Usually, friends, every week we do *Amor*. *Amor* means not ordinary love but Outrageous Love or Evolutionary Love.

- We live in a world of outrageous pain; the only response to outrageous pain is Outrageous Love.
- We live in a world of outrageous beauty; the only response to outrageous beauty is Outrageous Love.

By Outrageous Love, we don't mean ordinary love, which is a human predicament, all too often a strategy of the ego, a way to gain the upper hand, some security, some comfort—all of which are valid, but that's not what love is.

Love is not mere human sentiment. Love is the heart of existence itself.

Love is the Eros that pulses all of Reality, from the original sound waves in synchrony beyond imagination, to the dazzling expression of hundreds of billions of stars and a hundred billion neurons in the brain. The dazzling chorus of gorgeous, allured complexity that is always bringing separate parts together to form larger wholes, from the first nanoseconds of the Big Bang seeking ever more intimacy. From the deepest new sciences.

Reality is the progressive deepening of intimacies.

Wow! That's *Amor*. That's Outrageous Love.

AFTER THE CRUCIFIXION, THERE'S ALWAYS RESURRECTION

And so, every week we do this particular chant, *Amor*, but this week because it's Easter and to honor Easter, I want to share another chant, the *Ani*

Ma'amin chant. It's a chant which is about Easter. It's about looking in the face of death, in the face of hopelessness and knowing, with full trust that we're going to walk through.

There's a phrase that Barbara used to say and loved very much. She would call me almost every day and we would say this phrase to each other: *Are you ready to go all the way in this lifetime?* Let's make it more specific. *Are we ready to play a larger game? Are we ready to participate in the evolution of love? Are we ready to go all the way, right now?* This chant is about trust. It's about laughing in the face of death. I want to just share with you, just for a moment.

We've all touched death. We have friends who have died this year. We have friends who have died of Covid; we have friends who have died in other ways. We all feel the fragrance of death, because death is an intrinsic part of Reality.

> *But it's death that presses us into life. It's the knowing of death that makes us fully alive.*

Once we're in our aliveness, we have to access the realization—that Barbara's going to talk about, that I'm going to talk about from the perspective of the Tao, the interior and exterior science—**the realization and the actual knowing of living beyond death.**

That's what Easter is. Easter is the knowing that *after the crucifixion, there's always resurrection, that we are literally reborn*; that the notion of reductionist materialism that suggests that this life is all there is, is not science, is not rationalism. It's actually blind dogma that flies in the face of overwhelming evidence from the interior and exterior sciences.

By accessing that evidence—the evidence of the heart, the evidence of spirit, the evidence of classical data—we make different decisions. **Because we know we're not just deciding for now. We're deciding and creating our next step, our next incarnation in the continuity of consciousness.**

THE NEXT STEP IN CONSCIOUS EVOLUTION

NO MATTER WHAT IS GOING ON IN MY LIFE, I TRUST WITH COMPLETE TRUST

This chant that I'm about to share with you was sung by human beings who were walking to gas chambers in the middle of the Nazi Holocaust. Most of my family were among those who walked just a few decades ago. A mother holding her baby, a father holding his wife's hand, people alone, brothers and sisters.

And this is what they sang. They sang *ani ma'amin*, "I trust," *b'emunah she'leima*, "with complete trust," *be'vi'at ha'Moshiach*, "in the triumph of the new human." In the language of the lineage, Messiah is the new human.

V'af al pi she'yit'ma'mey'a, "even though She may tarry," even though the new human may tarry, She might not come, it's going to take a long time, we're waiting—but I know that I'm not *Waiting for Godot*, in Beckett's phrase— I'm actually actively waiting; I'm a full radical activist; I've emerged from *Homo sapiens* to *Homo amor*, and I'm the evolutionary human.

Im kol ze a'cha'ke lo, "nonetheless, I will wait."

Bechol yom she'yavo, "knowing that any day She may come."

I trust with complete trust.

No matter what's going on in my life, I trust with complete trust.

I trust with complete trust. No matter what's going on, I trust. This is what Barbara trusted in so gorgeously, in the coming of the new human and that we participate, that we generate that new human. No matter what's happening, *v'af al pi she'yit'ma'mey'a*, "even though so much breaks my heart, *Im kol ze a'cha'ke lo*, "I never resign myself." I never step back. I can sometimes get close. I can step back a little bit, but I never look away. I'm always waiting—and I'm never *Waiting for Godot*.

To wait for the Messiah means to become the Messiah, to become the new human, to become *Homo amor*.

Even if I'm walking towards the gas chamber, when it looks like power history has triumphed over *Homo amor*, I know that it's not true.

EVOLUTIONARY LOVE CODE: DEATH AND RESURRECTION ARE NATURAL EXPRESSIONS OF THE INTIMATE PATTERN OF REALITY

> When you find others to join genius with you, you contribute your unique note into the planetary awakening.
>
> You are being recorded and activated in the Book of Evolutionary Life.
>
> You become *Homo amor*.
>
> You are lived as a unique expression of LoveBeauty and LoveIntelligence of All-That-Is.
>
> Your Unique Self, *Homo amor*, joins the Unique Self Symphony, and the planet awakens as love. **Within that larger identity of *Homo Amor*, death and resurrection are natural expressions of the intimate pattern of Reality.**
>
> Our participation in the Unique Self Symphony is not exhausted within one lifetime but rather cuts across lifetimes.

Let's read this Evolutionary Love Code as an act of utter revolution, as an act of utter Renaissance.

Barbara's going to talk about the Unique Self Symphony and about Easter. And resurrection is not exhausted within one life but rather cuts across lifetimes. Barbara Marx Hubbard:

THAT'S US, ON THE ROAD TO THE PLANETARY AWAKENING IN LOVE

You know, I prayed for fulfilment for my life purpose, and I'll just pray for it with all of us. To place whatever that purpose is right now into the fullscale fulfilments of your entire life purpose of which that unique prayer is a component.

The glory of the fulfilment of life purpose together is the Unique Self awakening in love—which is the purpose of this church. When I began to think about this I was reminded of St. Paul on the road to Damascus— and he was out attacking the Jews, as you know. At some point, he had a complete, total experience of the resurrected Christ, who came to him and said, *Why are you putting all of these pricks into me? Why are you doing this?* St. Paul was completely blinded by the glory of what he saw. He came back. And this person who was persecuting the Jews became new—because he'd had a vision of the resurrected Christ.

I was thinking of all of us. We're calling for a Unique Self Symphonies vision. Maybe we've seen glimpses of it. **Maybe it has something to do with what the resurrected Christ is— a being that goes beyond the limitations of the current situation into a new being**, a new life, a new world.

So, I was thinking of St. Paul. I tend to deeply admire him because, finally, what he did is he started to walk and write letters—which reminds me of myself. I do emails! He writes these letters and what happens to the letters is that they form little churches.

At first, they form just little circles of people who were able to draw on the image of the resurrected Christ, which fulfils the story that he was crucified, he spent the three days in the tomb, and he came out as himself, but a new being. He didn't come out as a cosmic mystery. He came out, so he was recognized by Mary in the Bible. This story is exactly right.

If we pull ourselves forward and imagine that we are fulfilling our spiritual, our social, and our scientific, technological capabilities, we are exactly fulfilling the story of Christ.

DEATH IS NOT THE END OF THE STORY

Let's go back and see what happened in those early days and see what's happening now that could be related to that. Well, in the early days. Christ, Jesus, said something very strange before he went to die. Here is what he said: *Take, eat; this is my body. Take, drink; this is my blood given for you.* The most intimate expression: *Take, eat; this is my body, this is my blood.* Now, I used to know some Catholic Sisters. I once spoke to the Sisters of St. Joseph, and they called me a Catholic because I have this huge sense of expectancy. Well, the sense of expectancy is actually for the planetary awakening in love. That's the same thing as the resurrection and the eventual Second Coming of Christ.

So, all these small circles, what they did is they did communion. And I remember, because I was with the Catholic Sisters quite frequently, it had to be a priest. Only he could do it. He was all dressed up and they all went up one by one by one and they drank the wine, and they ate the wafer blessed as the body of Christ. The entire Catholic Church is eating the body of Christ, oh my God. So, I thought, *well, why not do that ourselves?* That was sacrilegious from a Catholic point of view. And we'll talk about this another time.

But I used to go around. I got a signal from God, *Take communion every day, Barbara*. I got a little knapsack, and I had a bottle of wine and crackers. I would visit friends, and I'd say, *would you like to do communion?* Nobody wanted to do communion, but I got them to do it anyway because I had the wafer and the wine and the crackers and the desire.

So we sat down, and we did it and we said, *Take, eat; this is the body of the living God that I am consuming inside myself to become like that by giving my voice in the Unique Self Symphony toward a planetary awakening in love*, which is comparable to what Jesus called for, the Christification of the earth. We're not using religious language because they have been narrowed—but we're certainly using the power of the story.

I would like to just conclude this by imagining together a Unique Self Symphony, everybody's voice. We're forming—in the Evolutionary Church—

gatherings of ourselves locally and globally, and the internet is our global nervous system. Let's be there right now, everybody. We've already prayed for what we want. Now we are gathering together on the global internet, on the nervous system of the planetary body experiencing, *Take, eat; this is the body and this is the blood of the living humanity*, that we are becoming by saying, *Yes, this is our body. This is our blood.*

I declare the celebration of giving our resources to this church. This is our body. This is our blood. Giving our resources for a planetary awakening in love through a Unique Self Symphony through this church being a premier voice on the entire planet and all of us incarnating a living body.

Do you realize St. Paul on the road to Damascus— that's us, on the road to the planetary awakening in love. This is the real thing. Our resources, our love, let it flow forth.

THIS IS THE REAL THING— WE LIVE BEYOND DEATH

This is the real thing and let's feel that and let's meet each other. Barbara, thank you so much. Let's just say thank you, Barbara, thank you. Huge thank you. Huge outpouring of thank you. With the thank you, to know *this is the real thing.*

And we commodify *the real thing.* Do you remember, growing up with the slogan, *It's the real thing.* Coke is? Really?

This is the real thing. This is what's real. It's not that *St. Paul did it and now it's over.*

> *We need to establish a universal grammar of spirit and value, which is the real thing, so we have a shared Reality story.*

Right now, we are faced with the loss of our future because we're facing the second shock: the death of humanity. We don't know how to arise, we don't know how to resurrect ourselves because we're lost in a global intimacy disorder.

And the global intimacy disorder is we don't have a shared sense of the real. Mathematics and engineering tell us *only they are real and the humanities, that's not real*. Then this religion says, *only we are real*. Then these people say, *only we are real. We are the real thing*. No! We participate together as the body of Christ. And the body of Christ is the body of the Universe.

- It's the body of Confucius.
- It's the body of the Buddha.
- It's the body of atman, which is Brahman.
- It's the body of Geist.
- It's the body of Mut.
- It's the body of the Eternal Logos.
- It's the body of the eternal, evolving Tao that we participate in directly.

We need to bring it all together in the greatest Renaissance revolutionary act in history, at this moment of second shock of existence, of death, as we're in these days moving towards resurrection. The resurrection will only happen when we have a shared story.

At the center of that shared story has to be the knowing that death is not the end of the story. I'm going to take a couple of minutes here, and this is huge, to actually know this and feel it.

> *I have to know that death is not the end of the story.*

So, let's do our second short sermon. We're going to put it together with Barbara's, and let's blow this away. Let's open up the space. Let's open heaven. Are we ready? We're ready to go the next step. We're here on this Easter. This is real, the Evolutionary Church, One Mountain, Many Paths. This is our revolution. We're on the road to Damascus and the road to Damascus is alive and well in us. I want to share an idea.

I want to read to you from the text of a great evolutionary mystic that I studied with Barbara. When we did Holy of Holies every week, we studied this evolutionary mystic together. His name is Abraham Kook and he writes, *It's necessary to explain the greatness of studying the secrets of Spirit. And the greatness is knowing the requirement to honor the inner knowings of the human being.*

Here in Evolutionary Church, in One Mountain, Many Paths, we call those inner knowings *anthro-ontology*. I remember when Barbara and I talked about this the first time, we were ecstatic. **Anthro-ontology means *the mysteries are within us.***

To know that we live beyond death, you can go in three different directions. They're all important. We're going to focus on the third.

> One direction we're not going to do today is to talk about dualism and materialism—the relationship between mind and body, what's called the hard problem of consciousness—and to show the five problems in materialism and the three major problems of dualism, to show why they don't work. Only a deeper understanding of the relationship between mind and body in which there's an actual continuity of mind, what I call "pan-interiority"—it's actually interiors and exteriors all the way up and all the way down—is the only way to understand Reality accurately. But we're not going to go in that direction. That's a different conversation.

We're not going to go in the way of the classical, important work of parapsychology. The evidence for reincarnation, for telepathy, for life after death, for neardeath experiences, for clairvoyance, for clairsentience. The evidence that the laws of physics don't exhaust Reality, and there's actually a nonlocal Reality, and there's a Reality in which **the continuity of consciousness is a demarcating feature of that Reality**. Our bodies are conduits for Spirit, but Spirit lives beneath and beyond the body. There's an enormous body of evidence that wasn't available 120 years ago that we've gathered carefully, starting with the important work of the British Psychical Society and then onto William James at the Harvard Society. We're not going to go in that direction.

Those are two important, critical directions to know how to move through death. We're not taking either of them right now. They're both important and we're going to be doing an entire book on death, which will ultimately encompass this. It's critical that we actually blow death out of the water but not by, as Google says, uploading ourselves to the web. Google has no idea how to do that because Google has no idea that there's a Self that's not computational. **When Google says, *upload yourself to the web*, when Ray Kurzweil talks about that, he talks about the human being as being reducible to computation.** That is a fundamental scientific error of the first order. It misunderstands what a human being is. It downgrades human beings and upgrades algorithms.

The way that we know, the way we understand that there's continuity of conscience, that we move beyond death, is anthro-ontologically. We're going to do something wild here in the next five minutes. If you're up for having an actual experience, let's have an experience of enlightenment, let's have an experience of knowing, let's have an experience of the Christ energy alive in us.

Let's become the wafer. Let's become the body of Christ. Let's do the Easter ceremony. Let's take communion in a new way.

Are we ready to take communion with our larger Selves, to take evolutionary communion, intimate communion with the larger frame of Reality?

EIGHT DOORS OF UNDERSTANDING TO THE CONTINUITY OF CONSCIOUSNESS

Here we go. I'm going to give you eight doors.

DOOR ONE: THE DOOR OF LONGING

The first door is longing.

You have, I have, we have **an anthro-ontological experience of inconsolable longing**.

And we think that we, as Wordsworth wrote, *exhaust* that longing.

It's a longing for music, it's a longing for beauty—but it's not exhausted.

> *Beauty and music are hints, directional signals, allusions to that for which we yearn.*

A fish doesn't yearn for dry land. We long for a larger and a deeper experience of life beyond the exigencies of this world because it's true. When there's a universal, inconsolable longing, it points to a fundamental truth.

We long for heaven.

It's easy to make fun of the Christians who talked about heaven with a lot of harps, but when they talked about heaven with a lot of harps, they weren't being silly. They were talking about a Reality in which it's all alright; a reality in which Goodness, Truth, and Beauty are the center; a Reality which is heaven.

We yearn for heaven. And I'm not talking about a mythical heaven; I'm not talking about a mythological heaven. I'm not talking about a premodern, ethnocentric, homophobic heaven. **I'm talking about a heaven that's a better place.** There's a better place to be **and we have an inconsolable longing for that better place to be**. That inconsolable longing itself is the anthro-ontological knowing that this world, this sublunar sphere, this vale of tears isn't all there is.

Who can find that? If you can find it, just find it inside in your body, and the body of Christ that lives awake and alive in you. *Who can find the inconsolable longing that lives alive in us?* If you can find it, cry out a *Yes!* We said last week we can be evangelicals. Not ethnocentric evangelicals but cosmocentric evangelicals! Sharing the good news in which no one is left out of the circle. That's our *Yes!*

So that's one. That's the first anthro-ontological gate. That's the first heaven's gate held in anthroontological truth. The mysteries are within us. *Yes!*

DOOR TWO: THE FEAR OF NOTHINGNESS IS THAT WHICH IS BEYOND NOTHINGNESS

Number two. We're doing enlightenment practice together, the enlightenment of knowing the truth beyond death. Find your fear of nothingness. Can you find that? Find the fear of just being obliterated when you die. *I die and I'm not there. Utter nothingness.* Who can find that fear? Just find the fear door. Stay deep. Don't go philosophical. Just find the raw fear in your body. Be direct, be honest, be authentic. Find it direct. Find it in your body—the utter fear of nothingness.

Now, if you can find that fear, you can dispel it and evaporate it. Because if nothingness were our nature, if we were, in fact, ultimately only dust to dust—we wouldn't fear nothingness.

That within us that fears nothingness is that which is beyond nothingness.

That within us that defies, that rejects nothingness is the eternity that lives in us, as us, and through us. We're afraid when we're told that it might be nothingness, because *all of us rebels*. The very fiber and fabric of our being rebels against this untruth. The fear of nothingness itself wouldn't be a fear.

The fear becomes an awareness. The fear of nothingness becomes the awareness of eternity. That's the second door. Now, if you can feel that for a second, then give us a, *Yes!* You can feel that your fear of nothingness, **your fear of nothingness itself is itself an indication, a door, an opening into eternity itself.** *Wow!*

The word in Hebrew for fear is *yir'ah*, "fear", but *yir'ah* also means "consciousness." To become conscious, to become aware. It's the deepest *dharma*. When I go into my fear and I follow my fear to its root—**at the root of the fear is awareness, is consciousness, is seeing.** *I can see clearly now the rain has gone.*

There is no nothingness, there's only *no-thingness*. There's eternity that's available. That is the fabric of Reality itself.

DOOR THREE: THE ETERNAL QUALITY OF TIMELESS TIME AND PLACELESS PLACE

Door three, oh my God, this is the door of True Self. **Have you ever experienced a moment in which time stood still?** It was so magnificent, it was so glorious that you could feel the quality of eternity in that time? As we've shared so many times together, eternity is not everlasting time. As Wittgenstein reminded us, *eternity is the timeless time*. It's the placeless place. Have you ever been in the embrace of the beloved and knowing, as you began to talk about love, that love is forever? **Have you ever experienced a moment of radical awe, radical amazement when you asked for wonder, and wonder disclosed itself and you felt the eternal quality?** When you rested in the divine embrace and the timeless time and the placeless place?

Find any one moment where you felt that quality of eternity and you know that that's the true quality of Reality and true Eros.

True eternity never disappears.

That's why we remember. We have a clear memory of every moment in our life, **every moment that we tasted eternity we can actually pull up in our** memory. And all the moments in which we were on the surface of time, we can't find.

Who can feel that? Who can find a moment like that?

Solomon writes *smolo tachat roshi,* "Your left hand is under my head," *vi-ymino t'chabkeni,* "Your right hand embraces me."

> *We are resting in this divine embrace, in this timeless time, in this placeless place.*

Let's rest in it. That's the third door. We know it. We feel it.

I had a moment like that with my son this past Thursday night. We were watching a movie together about this female warrior and he was resting in my arms. We looked at each other and we were just madly in love with each other. He went to visit his grandmother and grandfather, and we were at the airport on Friday. I looked him and I said, *Hey, I love you madly,* and he looked at me without artifice, just full young man. He says, *Dad, I love you madly. I'm going to miss you.*

That's eternity.

That moment never disappears.

That moment is a door, a portal to that timeless time and the placeless place.

So, we know that.

DOOR FOUR: INTUITION OF JUSTICE AND FAIRNESS

Let's go to four. The fourth anthro-ontological knowing of the continuity of consciousness, the knowing that consciousness is beyond the vagaries of this vale of tears, is fairness. I'm going to ask you a question, my friends. Do we not know so well this fourth way in which we knock at heaven's gate and open heaven's door? Do we not know that for so many people life doesn't actually work out fairly? How many of us know in our lives, dimensions of our lives where justice wasn't served in the course of one lifetime?

> ## Justice, fairness is an intrinsic quality of Cosmos itself.

I know that justice, that fairness, which every child intuits and says, *It's not fair, mom!*

It's got to be fair is inherent in our very body and being. Part of the body of Christ alive in us is a demand for the integrity of fairness, and we all know that it's not, for so many people, fair in one lifetime.

Can you feel that? Who can feel and know that for so many people, and for so many of us, it doesn't work out? There isn't an even distribution of joy, happiness, possibility, goodness and wisdom in one lifetime. Who knows that? We know that.

Which tells us, since we also know that Reality demands fairness, that integrity is the actual nature of Reality, that justice is the actual nature of Reality, that Lady Justice is the incarnation of She. When we know that, we know it can't be over in one lifetime.

It's self-evidently, anthro-ontologically true in our very body that *it can't be over in one lifetime. Wow!*

Who can feel that? Who can find that? Access it directly. You're having a direct experience of enlightened knowing and realization in this moment. *This is the real thing*, said Barbara. We are on the road to Damascus. We are flashing with the light that appears and blows open, and that light lives within us. *Wow!*

Ki imcha mekor ohr. b'orcha nir'eh ohr, "For with you is the source of light. In your light, we see light."

We know it inside of us: anthro-ontology. We knock on heaven's door, we open heaven's gate with the knowing that justice will be done, and it can't be done, it's not done, within the course of one lifetime.

DOOR FIVE: THE KNOWING OF THE HERO

Number five, let's knock. Are you ready to knock? *Kol dodee dofek*, "The voice of my beloved is knocking," writes Solomon in the Song of Solomon. The lover's on the other side of the door. And the lover is my enlightened Self; the lover is the sage and the seer that lives within me. But we get busy. The lover on the other side says, *Oh, I'm too busy.*

Pashateti et ku'ton'ti. I've taken off my garment. I'm in bed already. I've got to go, I don't have time to be enlightened. No!

> We're stepping in.
>
> We are the enlightenment.
>
> We are the light; it lives within us. There's not a sage and a seer *out there*.
>
> The sage and the seer lives inside of me.
>
> The body of Christ lives in me.
>
> The universal human lives in me.
>
> *Homo amor* lives in me.
>
> The Gnostic human lives in me.

It's the realization of the triumph of *Homo sapiens* as *Homo amor*.

Number five: the hero. Every culture knows the hero across time and space. Who knows the hero? Who recognizes the hero in your body? You can feel the hero.

And who is the hero?

> *The hero is the one who's willing to give up her life within this vale of tears for the sake of the larger intimate communion, for the sake of the larger whole.*

We know that that notion of the hero already comes alive in the animal world where an animal will sacrifice itself, literally.

The Universe: A Love story, for the sake of the larger whole.

Human beings, the greatest among us, have sacrificed themselves for the sake of the larger whole. But what does the hero know?

The hero knows that it's not over when it's over. The hero knows *my individual life is transcended. I don't disappear, but actually I become most alive at the moment of my death.*

And in that moment of death, I am reborn. The hero understands that *I participate in a larger field of value, and intimacy, and desire, and LoveIntelligence, and LoveBeauty, and LoveTruth.*

The hero experiences the mad love for the whole that allows the hero to transcend the limitation of this one lifetime into the larger value and the larger eternity. The hero knows, in the core of her being, that death is not real. It's the knowing of the hero. The hero is the early adopter of *Homo amor*. That's Door Five.

Through the hero, we knock on heaven's gate, we open heaven's door.

Who can feel that? Who can feel the knowing of the hero? We're talking about a hero who walks into the face of death. And the heroes are among us. Go to a scene that I've mentioned more than once before of *Saving*

Private Ryan, Tom Hanks movie. It's not about the Dalai Lama. It's about ordinary human beings. **The hero lives in every ordinary human being.**

The boys who landed on the beach of Normandy. The young men and women all over the world, medical professionals who risked their lives all through COVID without masks, with pizza boxes as a mask to heal the sick. Many of them died. And Italy's in lockdown again today on this Easter morning. So many heroes in Italy, so many heroes in France, so many heroes in Holland, so many heroes in Germany, so many heroes in India, so many heroes in the United States.

The hero lives in us. And the hero is the knowing of the continuity of consciousness.

DOOR SIX: THE EXPERIENCE OF UNIQUE SELF

Number six is Unique Self. Can we do it? Can we knock on heaven's door again? Are we willing to open heaven's gate a sixth time on this Easter morning in our evolutionary communion in which we become the wafer? We are the body of Christ. We're knocking on heaven's door. Number six is **the experience of my irreducible Unique Self**

- The knowing that I have a story.
- There's a plotline to that story.
- There's a journey that needs to be taken.
- I'm needed by All-That-Is.
- The plotline of my journey is chapter and verse in the journey of the Universe.

In the fractal essence of Reality—just as a fern contains within it the actual structure of the leaf, the tree, and the entire forest—**just as the fractal contains the whole, the individual Unique Self incarnates and embodies the whole**. My uniqueness is utterly needed. And we all know that our Unique Self doesn't exhaust itself within one lifetime.

Do you and I both know that's true? Do we know that we're actually not able to give all of our unique gift within one lifetime? Do we know that our uniqueness is somehow frustrated, that it can't be exhausted within a lifetime? Do we have a direct and clear experience of that truth in our very bodies? Do we know a thousand percent the full uniqueness of who I am?

Can you access that directly in your first-person experience, an anthro-ontological knowing? If we can access that right now, then we know. If you know the truth of Unique Self, then you know that …

> *Unique Self isn't exhausted in one lifetime.*

You have a direct experience of enlightenment in this second. You are Paul blinded by the light on the road to Damascus in this very second, right now, as you experience your Unique Self, right now, and understand that *it can't be exhausted in one lifetime*. You know the truth of your uniqueness, and you know the truth of the continuity of consciousness.

Oh my God, this is Easter Sunday. This is resurrection. Amen.

We're evangelicals. We're Jewish, and we're atheists, and we're Confucianists, and we're every kind of Buddhist, and we're every kind of Christian, and we're every kind of secular humanist, and we're all here together. **We're all here together in one intimate communion, in one global communion of pioneering souls.**

DOOR SEVEN: EITHER EVERYTHING'S MEANINGFUL OR NOTHING'S MEANINGFUL

Door seven is *either everything's meaningful or nothing's meaningful*; there's not a choice in between. Either life is *a tale told by an idiot full of sound and fury, signifying nothing*, and death is the sad, pitiful, withering end to that which was, ultimately and always, insignificant, or *tomorrow and tomorrow* and tomorrow creeps in this petty pace from day to day to the last syllable of recorded time,[6] in its glorious march to the crescendos of transformation and eternity. The timeless time and the placeless place live in us, as us, and through us, and death is not meaninglessness, but death is part of the larger fabric of meaning. Each one of us has an anthroontological knowing that the mysteries are within us.

> *How many of us know with absolute certainty that the premise that nothing is meaningful is absurd?*

How many of us know that? All of us know that! All of us live our lives every single day based on the common-sense sacred axioms. Common-sense means our common sensuality, the feeling in our body. *Through my body I vision God*, writes the Book of Job in Chapter 19, the common sensuality of my body coming alive.

I know there's meaning. If you can find one moment in your life that's meaningful, then that opens the door to all meaning because *either everything is meaningful or nothing's meaningful. Nothing is meaningful* is not a live option because each one of us can access directly one moment that's meaningful. **Once one thing is meaningful, then it's a field of meaning and then death is meaningful.** It's not meaningless. It's not the move into nothingness. Oh my God.

DOOR EIGHT: THE EXPERIENCE OF LOVING IS THE EXPERIENCE OF ETERNITY

Do you all remember Harry Chapin? I loved Harry Chapin. Harry Chapin is singing here for the knowing of every human being. He's not a philosopher. He knows this anthroontologically in his own being. Harry Chapin

---

6 William Shakespeare, *Macbeth, Act V, Scene V, lines 17–28*

had a song that I used to listen to all the time. Here it is. His song was *All My Life's a Circle*, and it goes something like this, the first couple lines:

> *All my life's a circle, sunrise and sundown.*
> *Moon rolls through the nighttime till the daybreak comes around.*
> *It seems like I've been here before, I can't remember when,*
> *but I have this funny feeling that we'll all be together again.*
> *I found you a thousand times, I guess you'd done the same,*
> *but when we lose each other, it's like a children's game.*
> *As I find you here again, a thought runs through my mind. Our love is like a circle, let's go around one more time.*

When you really love someone, you know that that love is forever.

That's the eighth knocking on heaven's door. We know in our bodies. The knowing that as soon as I truly love, I start using words like, *Forever. I love you. Will you be with me in the next lifetime? I love you forever.*

> ## *The genuine anthroontological experience of loving is the experience of eternity. It is the experience of "forever."*

Wow!

> *It seems like I've been here before, I can't remember when,*
> *but I have this funny feeling we'll all be together again.*

Yes. How many people can feel that and know that and access that directly? That's not a myth. That's not an illusion. I know the continuity of consciousness, and I know it is an absolute truth and absolute reality. We don't have *certainty* about how it works. It's not owned; that's a false certainty. We don't have certainty about when and where and the details and the precision of it. We don't know all of that. That's uncertainty. But what we know is that there's continuity of consciousness. We know it's not over when it's over.

We know that everything's meaningful. We know that when we knock on heaven's door, heaven's door opens. We know that our inconsolable yearning and longing is not absurd, but rather the truest index, of our truest situation and so, therefore, we can trust.

C.G. Jung, the great philosopher, writes in one of his lesserknown writings, *I can't establish psychological stability, mental depth, with a patient until they know of immortality.* Wow!

Until we know the truth of the continuity of consciousness, we're lost in *a tale told by an idiot* that ultimately all of its *sound and fury* ceases at death's door and, therefore, it ultimately *signifies nothing.* Wow!

We trust.

Even as my relatives walked into the gas chambers, even as all of the forces of tragedy conspired against them, they breathed with their last breath the radical trust in the new human. For them, for my ancestors and your ancestors, for all of our ancestors—because we're all part of the same ancestors—and for all our descendants:

- We're going to stand today against existential risk.
- We're going to stand against the second shock of existence, which is the death of humanity.
- We're going to stand for the larger truth of the continuity of consciousness and for the creation of heaven on earth through the articulation of a new story, a story of Unique Self, of planetary awakening in love through Unique Self Symphonies.
- We're going to stand for a planetary Pentecost—together with you, Barbara.

I trust with complete trust. For all the heroes. It's you. It's all about you. It's about your Unique Self. It's about your gift. It's about your stepping up. Reality desperately needs you and is madly in love with you and we're madly in love with each other.

CHAPTER THREE

WHY LEVELS OF CONSCIOUSNESS MATTER: THE GREAT STORY OF EVOLUTIONARY DEVOTION

Episode 263 — October 24, 2021

THE NEW STORY OF VALUE IS OUR NEW HOME

Every week our intention, in this time between stories, in this time between worlds, is to participate in the evolution of love.

We are erotic mystics. By erotic we mean not only a particular expression of Eros which is the sexual. **By erotic we mean that which is underneath the sexual, the Eros that drives all of Reality.** You can be radically erotic and celibate, or you can be having sex all the time and be completely non-erotic. We're talking about Eros.

An erotic mystic is one who understands that my desire is the desire of evolution, my Eros is the Eros of evolution, awake and alive in me.

An erotic mystic understands that we are evolution awakening to itself uniquely in us.

When Barbara—my beloved whole mate and friend and evolutionary partner who I miss dearly—when Barbara Marx Hubbard and I sat together right before she died in

Portland, we drew The Wheel of Co-Creation 2.0 on a napkin. Barbara had originally done something called The Wheel of Co-Creation. Then Barbara and I created a new wheel called Wheel 2.0.

One of the major shifts we made is that at the very center of this Wheel, which is a Venn diagram of Reality itself, **we placed desire—not surface desire, but your Deepest Heart's Desire.** Because my Deepest Heart's Desire is the desire of the evolutionary impulse itself, awake and alive in me.

So, at this time between worlds, this time between stories, when we're confronted with existential risk and catastrophic risk, when we're confronted with pandemic, we're confronted with a kind of fundamental instability, we have to actually begin to find home again and create a new home. That home comes from the realization of a new story; a new story that integrates the best validated insights of premodern, modern, and postmodern wisdom into a greater whole, a new Story of Value rooted in First Principles and First Values. That's the only way I can come home.

That births a new narrative of identity, a new story of who I am.

Who am I?

- I'm the personal face of the evolutionary impulse.
- I'm a unique configuration of the desire that drives all Reality.
- I'm a unique quality of intimacy.
- I'm God's unique intimacy.
- I'm God's unique desire.

Not as a slogan, not as a declaration, but an actual lived realization of the nature of who I am. Because that's what enlightenment means.

We need to democratize enlightenment. Of course there are levels of attainment, but enlightenment must be a genuine option for every human being.

It's only from that place of this new identity that I can actually begin to act for the sake of the whole. In this new identity I actually realize that

I'm God's unique intimacy, I'm God's unique desire, I'm a unique configuration of intimacy and desire, I'm a unique expression of the evolutionary impulse, I'm taking my place in the Unique Self Symphony—

And I realize that the whole lives in me.

And I can be omni-considerate of the whole.

And I can begin to heal the horrifically fractured Cosmos, lost in a devastating global intimacy disorder, which is the root cause for all of the generator functions of existential risk.

EVERY HUMAN BEING HAS THE RIGHT TO DESIRE AND TO BE DESIRED

One First Value and First Principle of Cosmos is desire. Desire is not just political; last week, we looked at my colleague, Amia, who wrote her book on *The Right to Sex*. But the point of the book is that there is no right to sex, there's no right to desire. Of course, when she talks about it, she's talking about something very limited. She caricatures and sets up a straw man and kills it and says *There's no right to desire*, in the sense of, *I have a right to desire you or to have sex with you*. No, it's never specific. Of course that's not true.

But there's a general, meta, essential, personal right to desire and to be desired. It's not just political. **Underneath politics is something deeper, and that which is deeper are the First Principles and First Values that politics emerges from.**

Now imagine for a second, as we set our intention this week, that every human being in the world had the radical joy of being desired. It's a fundamental human need and a fundamental human right: to desire and to be desired. Not simply surface desire but clarified desire; to actually desire your Deepest Heart's Desire.

That's what it means to wake up as Conscious Evolution.

EVOLUTIONARY LOVE CODE: WAKE UP, GROW UP, SHOW UP

We're born awake; we fall asleep. This is the intention of Cosmos.

The purpose of Reality is to wake up, but that is not enough. I must wake up, grow up, and show up.

Wake up means an expanded state of consciousness in which I realize my true nature, your true nature, and the true nature of all of Reality. Waking up, however, is somewhat like feminine values or God; they don't take you home.

Now that's a provocative but crucial sentence. To explain: waking up is mediated through the prism of growing up. We have to wake up, we have to find God, and we have to integrate feminine values at the higher levels of consciousness. That's what takes us home. Only then, after waking up and growing up, can I realize that the purpose of my life is to show up as my Unique Self and participate in the Unique Self Symphony.

If there's a single code that can change the world, it's this one, and this is our topic.

But just to prepare, to be ready, to find ourselves, and to go one step deeper, we reach beyond, and we realize that *we're not the only actors. We're not alone on the stage.* We realize that we're always being carried, and we're always being held. We recognize the gorgeousness and elegance and dazzling beauty of the third-person of Reality that flows through Cosmos.

My friend and colleague—a kind of spiritual friend; we're doing the same work, we've only exchanged a few emails—Brian Swimme talks beautifully about the third-person of the Divine, of goodness that flows through Cosmos. As do his teachers, Thomas Berry and Mary Evelyn Tucker, people who are working on the Universe story. Then we have our Buddhist friends. I, myself, have been honored to do a lot of teaching of that nature, although not through the Buddhist prism, but through the interior sciences of Western mysticism, which is first-person: *She lives in me.*

But at the core is second-person, which means that not only does She live in me, not only does she flow through Reality in all the laws and manifestation of physics and the four forces and all the fields, but actually, She's holding us in Her arms and She's saying, *You're my baby*.

There's something unbelievably gorgeous when someone looks at you and says, *You're my baby*. It doesn't matter how old we are. ***You're my friend, and I love you madly. I'm holding you. Wherever you fall, you fall into my hands.***

That's not a dogma; that's a realization. To know the difference between the two is everything. Let's close our eyes for a second. **Let's feel into the second-person, the personhood of Cosmos, which is not a dogma but a realization.** God or Divinity. Remember, the god you don't believe in doesn't exist, not the caricatured God, not the cosmic vending machine god.

The God who is the incessant creativity of Cosmos, the God who is *tat tvam asi*, who lives in you, as you, and the through you, and the God who knows your name and holds you, the God who is the Beloved. Let's just feel it together.

THE FIELD OF INTELLIGENCE HEARS YOU TALKING

When I ask you *Do you hear my voice*, you say *Yes*. Then I ask you *What in you hears my voice*, and you say, *My ears*. I say, *Well, it's not just your ears; ears are physical apparatus, but what animates your ears? There's an intelligence, a consciousness. So, your intelligence and consciousness hear me talk.*

Now, I know you're a fantastic person, and I know you're really smart and intelligent and really conscious. But just between you and me, are you the most intelligent person in the whole state, in the whole country, in the whole world? Probably not.

So, if your intelligence hears me, could it be that your intelligence is the only intelligence that hears me?

Is it true is that your intelligence is just you?

Is your intelligence separate from the larger field of intelligence?

Is your consciousness separate from the larger field of consciousness?

If you can hear me talking, is it possible that the field of intelligence and consciousness can't hear me talking? Of course not.

So, **just as you hear me and just as I hear you, the field of intelligence and consciousness**—from which neither you nor I are in any way separate—**hears me.**

That's the experience of prayer.

Prayer means that no words are lost.

Prayer means that no one dies alone.

Prayer means that we may live lives, sometimes, of quiet desperation, but we're never ultimately lonely, because we're never alone; we're always held, and we always fall into Her arms. She is the Infinity of Intimacy that knows our name and holds our holy and broken Hallelujah.

Every week we practice this not as information. As Dogen said when asked by his students, *why do you meditate?* He said, *that's what Buddhists do.*

I meditate like I breathe.

I realize personhood.

I say, *I love you and you love me.*

Because that's the act of realization; it's the act of being alive.

To be loved and to love is self-evidently meaningful; it needs no other justification.

We realize that we both participate in and we're held by the Infinity of Intimacy that knows our name. It doesn't matter whether you call that Infinity of Intimacy, Ma'at, or Geist, or the Implicate Order, or Christ, or the Buddha Field, or any of the names of the Hindu goddesses: Lakshmi or Kali, Shiva or Shakti, Sita or Rama. It doesn't matter whether it's Earth or Sky.

> *It's the personhood of Cosmos, more intimate, closer to you than you can imagine; caring, desperately, madly, tenderly desiring you in every second.*

We offer on the altar before She, who's holding us right now, our holy and our broken *Hallelujah*. We do it anew every week and offer up our holy and our broken *Hallelujah*.

THE PURPOSE OF REALITY IS TO WAKE UP AND TO GROW UP

Let's look at the code. Here's the code once more:

> We're born awake; we fall asleep. This is the intention of Cosmos. The purpose of Reality is to wake up, but that is not enough. **I must wake up, grow up, and show up.**
>
> Wake up means an expanded state of consciousness in which I realize my true nature, your true nature, and the true nature of all of Reality. Waking up, however, is somewhat like feminine values or God; they don't take you home.
>
> Now that's a provocative but crucial sentence. To explain, waking up is mediated through the prism of growing up. We have to wake up, we have to find God, and we have to integrate feminine values at the higher levels of consciousness. That's what takes us home. Only then after waking up and growing up, can I realize that the purpose of my life is to show up as my Unique Self and participate in the Unique Self Symphony.
>
> *We're born awakened; we fall asleep. This is the intention of Cosmos.*

It's not a mistake that we fall away. We never actually fall away, but we experience ourselves as falling asleep. The purpose of Reality is to wake up.

But it's not enough to wake up. Wake up means an expanded state of consciousness. So, a state is like a drunken state: it comes, it's there, and then it's gone. Or a psychedelic state, or a state of rage, or a mystical state.

A state is a focused realization, where I'm completely inside something and I experience it fully, and then it's gone.

In a wake-up state, I realize my true nature and the true nature of Reality. But that's not enough; a wake-up state won't take you home.

We say in the code, *neither waking up, nor feminine values will get you anywhere.* Just as waking up will get you nowhere, just as God will get you nowhere. Because waking up isn't sufficient.

Your state of waking up has to be mediated through the prism of growing up.

That's we're going to talk about today.

WAKE UP STATES ARE NOT ENOUGH

It's a very deep idea that was core to the interior sciences of Hebrew wisdom. It's a core notion that you can have a prophetic experience, where you're completely blown open. But your experience of being blown open to the true nature of Reality is mediated through a prism—through the prism of your psychological maturity, through the prism of your socio-cultural experience, and as we now understand even more deeply, *through the prism of your level of consciousness.*

Let's say you could have feminine values, but you have a low level of consciousness. So, you are a mother who raises her children to fight for the Taliban; you could be a mother who raises her children to join Hitler

Youth. You've got these feminine values: you're nurturing, you're caring, you're empathetic. But your care, your nurture, and your empathy are at an ethnocentric level: *it's us versus them, we're inside and they're outside*—and you're contributing to evil.

So, you don't need feminine values. It's not about God. It's not about waking up. It's about:

- *At what level of consciousness*—or let's call it what level of growing up—*does your wakeup happen?*
- At what level of growing up do you experience God?
- At what level of growing up do you experience feminine values?

I'm going to tell you something wild. There're two conversations.

One that I had last night, which was a really important conversation with someone who's just enormously precious to me as a human being. Then I had another conversation a few days ago with another person who's just close to me in a different way, a different relationship, but a fantastic human being whom I love dearly.

The second one I just described was a Holy of Holies session, and with his permission, I'm going to share a little bit about what we talked about. I'm going to reflect on this conversation I had last night, and I want to do it in the following context. It's going to be funny, but it's wildly important and wildly beautiful. Let's start with funny.

Last week someone wrote me and said, "Wow, why is Krista—and this week it was Barbara Marx Hubbard—talking to people and saying, *let's pour resources and funds and become a member into One Mountain*? I come here for this deep transmission, spirituality, and love. So why are we asking for money, why are we asking people to become members? That's such a turnoff." So, I got an email like that—and I get one every once in a while.

THE NEXT STEP IN CONSCIOUS EVOLUTION

You saw how beautifully Barbara Marx Hubbard, together with Krista, invited people to become members this week.

Because we can't make this revolution, we can't be at this time between worlds and time between stories and participate in the evolution of the source code, which is the evolution of culture and consciousness, without understanding this mystery.

I've got to wake up, my wake up is mediated through the prism of my grow up, and only then can I show up as my Unique Self and participate in the Unique Self Symphony.

I want to talk specifically about this email I got, about this Holy of Holies I had, where a very dear close person said, *what should I do next, am I done, what's my next step, what do I need?* Then my conversation last night.

I have a friend who is a minister of a Catholic Church in a parish in Harlem. Just between us, my friend is not a really good minister. So, he got fired, and then they hired someone else—and this is about 20 years ago—he wasn't such a good minister, and they've hired someone else. The leadership just really wasn't great, and there were all sorts of financial challenges—**but people kept supporting the parish.**

I loved the parish. I used to go there 20 years ago, and it is still thriving today!

So let me ask you a question. Why is that parish thriving? Why are people supporting this Catholic parish with lousy ministers and bad leadership? It just keeps going on. Someone new comes and they pick up the baton. Why is that happening?

THE GREAT STORY OF EVOLUTIONARY DEVOTION

In the New Age world, we're afraid of words like devotion, sacrifice, commitment, loyalty, sincerity.

Those are scary words. Those are words that have to do with "them." We're free, autonomous, and independent.

That is why the New Age world, and the human potential world don't create structures of radical commitment that stand and that build, that would have the capacity to evolve the source code of culture and consciousness.

Because people at that level of consciousness where human potential and New Age lives, are somewhat narcissistically absorbed in their own journey. *This is my hero's journey. This is my story. How does this serve me right now? How is this addressing my needs?*

Now, those are all important; those are important emergent levels of consciousness, and those are all really good questions, but they're dissociated from a larger field, and they don't make space for devotion, for loyalty, for God, for sacrifice, and for commitment.

Those are all wake up words:

- I wake up to this experience of devotion.
- I wake up to this experience of loyalty as a core structure of Cosmos.
- I wake up to an experience of reverence.
- I wake up and I feel my sincerity.

All those experiences, all those qualities, and all those states that I can be in—all of those are mediated through a level of consciousness.

So, there's no such thing as devotion, there's no such thing as feminine values, there's no such thing as God, there's no such thing as commitment, there's no such thing as sacrifice, there's no such thing as reverence, there's no such thing as loyalty—there's loyalty *at a particular level* of consciousness. There's no such thing as love—there's love *at a particular level* of consciousness. There's devotion *at a particular level* of consciousness.

Let's walk through this.

DEVELOPMENTAL LEVELS OF CLARE GRAVES

Let's take Clare Graves. He is a colleague of Abraham Maslow, and he's one of the important developmentalists. His student Don Beck took Clare Graves's work and created a contemporary system called Spiral Dynamics, which is a quite well-known system. Ken Wilber then popularized that system.

But let's go back to Clare Graves, who talks about his system as a **biophysical cultural system**. He talks about six levels, from Graves level one, all the way to Graves level six.

We're going to do all six Graves levels. This is core to the Unique Self work of Unique Self Institute that our Claire Molinard is working on. It's core to everything that's happening.

I want to run through this in a really beautiful way, and we're going to see why this matters. It changes everything. Later, Chris Cowan, Don Beck, who were students of Clare Graves, attached colors to these levels, so I'm going to use their colors.

1. Graves level one is clan (Beige).

We are looking here not at Spiral Dynamics but Clare Graves's work. I'm doing pre–Spiral Dynamics. Let's assign a movie to each one, just for the heck of it; we'll make it up as we go. *The Clan of the Cave Bear*. So, it's a very small clan, your goal is survival. Of course, there's spirit and there are dimensions of religion and there's value, but it's a very closed insular circle, and the major goal is survival. There's a more limited sense of time, because we're concerned with survival, and that's our focus. That's the first level.

There's depth, there's nuance, there's lots of beauty. **The fundamental thrust is the survival of the clan.**

- It's close.
- It's intimate.
- It's focused on survival.
- It's completely related to the immediate experience of people with each other.
- Everyone knows each other.
- Values and ethics are completely immediate in their interpersonal nature.

It's a very, very small clan—150 people or less, usually less than what's called the Dunbar number (Robin Dunbar, the British anthropologist). That's Beige: *Clan of the Cave Bears*.

2. Graves level two is tribal (Purple).

Purple is tribal. The tribe is much bigger, bigger than the Dunbar number. You're connected to the tribe through bloodlines. *Do you have the right blood, or do you not have the right blood? If you have the right blood, you're in.* There's a lot of magic and ritual and shamanism, and perhaps prayer. The goal is the tribe. It's a local goal. The tribe is not universal; it's *from that mountain to that river*. The shaman is responsible in a way that he received perhaps from his father for that area.

- We propitiate the gods to help us.
- The values are the values of the tribe.
- **Loyalty of the tribe is paramount.**
- Knowing the magical arts that bring about healing and victory is essential.

That's the tribe. At the level of tribe, we begin to move from hunter gatherer—hunter gatherer is more the Beige—into tribal. Hunter gatherers are also tribe, but tribe that also allows for farming. **The tribe moves into agriculture; the tribe gets a larger sense of time.** That's Purple.

3. Graves level three is Power (Red).

Red is straight power; Thrasymachus in Plato's Republic. *Might makes right*; it's the drive for power.

- It's not just about loyalty to the tribe.
- It's not just about the survival in the clan.
- **It's the value of power itself.**
- It's this drive to power.

Attila the Hun is not just about the Huns, he's about power. It's this raw power drive that moves in Cosmos underneath lots of other disguises. So, you've moved from Purple to Red, which is this conquest in power. That's Graves level three.

4. Graves level four is mythic membership (Blue).

Blue is mythic membership: the Catholic Church, the Holy Roman Empire.

This is a whole new level of consciousness, in which it's not about the bloodlines of the tribe.

It's not about the loyalty to the 150 people at Graves level one, Beige.

It's not Purple, which is loyalty to the tribe and the bloodlines.

It's not Red, which is the power drive.

It's Blue, which is, *we're all part of a same system*—we're part of the Holy Roman Empire, we're part of the Christian church, we're part of a universal Islam—*and anyone can join.*

You don't have to be from that particular bloodline; if you adopt those principles you can join.

- There's a desire to conquer the world, but for the sake of not just power but to spread these ideas. Alexander the Great wants to spread Hellenism throughout the world.
- You can "become" a Hellenist, so there's the capacity to join.

- There's the beginning of universal principles, but those universal principles are held and understood and interpreted only by this empire or by this church.

Now, if you don't join, you're damned to hell. If you don't join the Holy Roman Empire, you're a barbarian and you can be slaughtered. But there's the possibility of joining, **there's a movement towards essential principles: coming from bloodline, it's now the emergence of the empire, the world religions.** That's Blue. That goes pretty much through the Renaissance, all the way till the Western Enlightenment. Beginning in the Renaissance, moving through the Western Enlightenment, we merge into Graves level five, which is Orange.

5. Graves level five is about the individual (Orange).

Orange is already about the individual, the separate self.

The separate self has value independent of the clan (Graves level one, Beige), of the tribe (Graves level two, Purple), and of the mythic membership (Graves level four, Blue).

- The individual per se has rights.
- It's the beginning of universal human rights.
- It's the beginning of achievement and meritocracy—independent of any Empire, independent of any tribe, and independent of any organized religion. You have rights, per se.

We begin to extrapolate from all the information we have in Cosmos to universal principles. They're not mediated through a particular kingdom or through a particular Empire or a particular tribe.

That is rational; that is an achievement. That is the Western Enlightenment.

It is Graves level five. But the weakness of the Western Enlightenment was that this sense of universal human rights left women out, and left the gay community out, and left LGBT out, and left native communities out. This notion of universal human rights pretty much applied to British men who own land. It left a lot of people outside of the circle.

6. Graves level six is pluralistic (Green)

So we went from Graves level five (Orange) to Graves level six (Green), which is:

- Multicultural
- Pluralistic
- Honoring the indigenous, honoring the native
- Sensitive to the hidden victims
- Deeply sensitive to the hidden power motives that are disguised in the narratives of Orange and the narratives of Blue

The earlier levels, Blue and Orange, have stories, but those stories are often hiding Red, which is raw power drives. So, we become aware of those power drives.

So, Green is postmodern. Think about certain communities in Holland and certain communities in Boulder, Colorado or San Francisco, or parts of England. **It's a universal consciousness: multicultural, pluralistic.**

So, *values are relative, they're a point of view, but they're beautiful, and everyone's got to be included in them.* That's Graves level six. That's where most of the liberal community lives today.

THE EXPERIENCE OF COMMITMENT AT DIFFERENT LEVELS OF CONSCIOUSNESS

All of those are called "first tier."

First tier means that you live predominantly at one of those places, or even two of them. A person could be both Blue and Orange: both part of Blue, mythic membership, deep Catholic, complete, committed, and Orange, also a rational achiever.

I live at one or two of those levels of consciousness, and that's where I interpret the world.

Now, at Blue—classical Catholic, for example, or Jewish, or French Patriot—I'm completely committed to take care of my church. If I'm a good Catholic in Harlem at a Blue level of consciousness, I understand that I've got a commitment, an obligation, and a responsibility to perpetuate the church. That's obvious. If I'm a patriot at, let's say, the Orange level—I'm German, or I'm French, or I'm English—even though I'm not part of the church, I'm part of this nationality, and I'm committed to that nationality, because I know I've got to perpetuate it and I've got to go to war for it. Even though I'm a citizen of the world, I'm also a citizen of my country. I'm committed to that, and that's a real commitment.

Those commitments can be beautiful. But if the religion is corrupt, then those commitments can be corrupted. If the nationality is corrupted, those commitments can be corrupted.

- So, loyalty, devotion, my experience of God, all of that appears in a particular way at Graves level one, when I'm in a clan.
- It all appears in a completely new and different way if I'm part of a tribe.
- Then they appear in a different way if I'm part of an empire or a great organized religion.
- They appear in a different way if I'm a citizen of the world; rational.
- If I'm an achiever, then my experience of God is completely different.

My experience of self, my experience of God, my experience of loyalty, my experience of devotion—those all are completely different at every level of consciousness.

All this is the first tier of Reality, in which I live primarily in one of those levels of consciousness, or in two together.

"BECOME A MEMBER" MEANS SOMETHING DIFFERENT AT EACH LEVEL OF CONSCIOUSNESS

So, when someone asks for support and says *become a member*—"become a member" means something particular. Let's say:

At Blue: *Become a member of the Catholic Church, but if you don't, you're burning in hell. Become a member of the Catholic Church, because if you don't, you've got no way to heaven. Become a member of the Catholic Church because we have the only way.*

That's one kind of membership.

At Orange: *Become a member of a certain kind of conformist society.* At Orange, we conform: we go to Wall Street, we dress in a certain way.

At Green, I might conform to being a certain kind of hippie, New Age-y person. I'm adopting and supporting that particular way of being, but *I don't realize* I'm doing it. I think I'm choosing, but I'm not choosing at all.

I can become a member, or I can be in devotion in a different way at every level of consciousness.

We've exiled devotion, loyalty, sacrifice, contribution, because we think those are all Graves level four (Blue), or at best, they're Graves level five (Orange) where you're committed to your company in some way.

When we get to Green, the classical liberal place, we let go of devotion and loyalty; **we think that's a lower level of conscious:** *maybe that's Red, the mafia. I'm part of a magical tribe, that's where loyalty belongs*—that's a mafia virtue. Devotion? Devotion is for those benighted old religious people who believe in those dogmas. Sincerity? I'm going for creativity, not sincerity. Reverence? Reverence, that's also Graves level four (Blue).

Now, that's all not true. All of those qualities live at every level of consciousness:

- We need to be devoted, but we need *evolutionary* devotion.
- We need commitment, but we need *evolutionary* commitment.
- We need loyalty, but we need *evolutionary* loyalty.
- We need love, but we need *evolutionary* love.

This means I'm now second tier, and I'm experiencing that I'm waking up from *Homo sapiens* to *Homo amor*.

Each one of these is a level of consciousness, is my experience of waking up, is my experience of feminine values, is my experience of God, is my experience of loyalty, is my experience of devotion, is my experience of sincerity.

All of those experiences are all qualities of waking up. They're all mediated through the prism of growing up, which is my level of consciousness.

This particular model—Graves level one (Beige), Graves level two (Purple), Graves level three (Red), Graves level four (Blue), Graves level five (Orange), Graves level six (Green) —that's all first tier.

FROM TIER ONE TO TIER TWO

The huge jump is when I go to second tier. When I go to second tier, I realize that, number one, for the first time *I can actually see the spiral*. Even if we've talked about it before, you might see it anew or you might be seeing it for the first time; you can actually *see* the six levels.

When you can see the six levels for the first time, you've jumped to second tier.

Number two, you see that all six of these levels live in you:

So you have a *magic* side.

You have a *commitment to your tribe*, whether it's your religion, or you might be a gang member, or it's this radical commitment to your particular community.

You're also an *achiever*. You might be *part of a great religion*. Or you might also be Green pluralistic; you want to be completely *inclusive of everyone*.

You could have all of the spiral live in you, and you become aware that it's all in you.

1. Second tier, you can see the spiral.
2. It all lives in you.
3. You can elegantly—as a Jedi Knight, if you will, or as a knight of Spirit, as an awakened what we call *Homo amor*—you can move between levels of the spiral.

So you can access your business rational achiever side, which is about universal human rights, your own achievement, production; it's about rationality. But you can also access your magical side, which is Purple, in your tribal sense. Sometimes you've got to access Beige, which is just raw survival. At other times, you might be deeply committed to a world religion in a particular way; or you might be deeply into Graves level six (Green): indigenous, pluralistic, with a certain kind of sensitivity and a certain kind of inclusiveness.

They all live in you, and you can move between them.

THE JUMP FROM FIRST TIER TO SECOND TIER

When I jump to second tier, where I can see the whole spiral...

- I realize that I've got to wake up.
- I realize that waking up is going to be mediated through my

- level of consciousness.
- ♦ I realize that I've got to synergize different dimensions of devotion and bring them all together in a higher level into evolutionary devotion.

So yes, I give money, of course I do. That's why that parish is still going in Harlem—because that parish in Harlem has got this level of consciousness which is Blue. But here's the big key.

So fare we looked at three dimensions of second tier. Now, here's the fourth and the most important one:

> *Second tier **transcends and includes** all the best qualities of all the previous levels.*

I've got to take the best of Blue, the best of Red: power, and the best of Orange: achievement, and the best of Green: pluralistic, and the best of Purple: magical and loyalty to my family bloodline, and the best of Beige: raw survival.

I've got to take the best of all those levels of consciousness, synergize them, and integrate them into a new story, into a new level of consciousness, which is second tier.

So, I *claim* devotion, I *claim* contribution, I *claim* sacrifice, I *claim* commitment together with autonomy, freedom, personhood, and creativity. They live together at second tier.

One Mountain is yours, One Mountain is ours. There's no way we can build One Mountain without contribution; it's not going to happen. If we think, when we start talking about contribution, *that's antiquarian, that's regressive, that's the religions, that's not what we do, we come here and be spiritual.* . . No! No!

We have no chance—at this moment between dystopia and utopia, in this time between worlds, when we're holding the keys to the new source code, and we're working day and night together to evolve the source code of culture and consciousness—**we have zero chance of being successful unless we sacrifice, unless we are committed.**

In other words, we all take a stand at the level that's comfortable to us.

If we don't put ourselves on the line, if we are not committing then it's never us, we're not on the line. We think…

It's the project, I support it from a distance.

It doesn't really hurt me; it gives me something good and I'm okay.

And I'm loving,

…but I never put myself on the line. It's theirs, I'm in support. I'm not on the line—that's uncomfortable. **It's uncomfortable to be on the line:**

I don't want to sacrifice at that level.

I don't want to be committed at that level.

I don't want to be devoted at that level.

I don't want to be loyal at that level.

I don't want to be sincere at that level.

That's too much.

Well, that doesn't work! That is a recipe for failure.

So, in our devotion, we're not devoted to the teacher, and we're not devoted to the structure of a particular mythic organization.

We're devoted to the vessel of One Mountain that allows us to accomplish our mission.

We've got to be *radically* devoted. I'm radically devoted. Are you? I'm radically loyal. I want to be as sincere as I can be. I want to hold every single person here in reverence. I'm devoted to every single person here.

THE GREAT STORY OF EVOLUTIONARY DEVOTION

But we're devoted together to the larger vision; *it's an evolutionary devotion.* But it's not less real, it's not less radical than those people who kept the parish going in Harlem, even though this minister wasn't so good and that minister wasn't so good, and there was this problem and that problem. But they showed up and they made contributions, and they gave money; they gave money at a level that it actually hurt. *I'm actually going to impact my life. I'm not going to make this sanitized, convenient.*

A guy named Todd Slater talked about The Toilet Assumption of the Western world: Anything that's kind of like manure, instead of letting it fertilize, we flush it down out of the way, meaning **we don't want the challenges in our face of what it takes to fertilize and grow the new world.** It's like, whoa, that's too much! So, we flush that away.

We want to be comfortable. We want to be safe. We want to be sanitized.

But friends, that's not how it works!

- It's agony and ecstasy.
- It's wonder and radical amazement.
- It's not just about my self-development.
- It's not just about where I am.

There's only one question we ever have to answer: *What does Reality need from me at the next moment?* **What it needs from me is not just my next experience:** Not just my next high. Not just my next state of consciousness. Not just my next experience of waking up.

Not just my next devotion to a mythic god at the Graves level four (Blue) as part of my local church or local synagogue. No!

Reality needs me to be in service to the Field of Evolution itself.

I'm animated by Outrageous Love. Outrageous Love is Evolutionary Love. I'm animated by evolutionary devotion, by evolutionary commitment, by evolutionary sacrifice—and none of that obfuscates my freedom. Because my freedom is not *freedom to do whatever I want.*

It's not your life. Why do you think it's your life? Did you choose when to be born? Did you choose to whom to be born? Did you choose where to be born? Why would you think it's your life? **It's our life together.**

You can't be sitting in a boat saying, *I'm going to drill a hole under my part of the boat because it's my part of the boat.* We're in this boat together. We need each other.

It's our life, and we're in service to the whole.

When we're in service to the whole,

- then we individuate in our Unique Self
- then we're fulfilled
- then our wake-up is mediated through the highest possible stage of consciousness: a radical growing up as a Unique Self participating in Unique Self Symphony—omni-considerate, madly in love, for the sake of the whole.

That's what we're trying to do. That's our goal. That's our vision. That's why we ask for contribution. We ask for contribution because we have to include that level of loyalty and devotion that Graves level four (Blue) knew: the utter commitment to the local parish. We've got to be much more than that. We can never be less than that.

CHAPTER FOUR

CELEBRATING THE COURAGE TO EVOLVE: BEYOND THE DARK SHADOWS OF TRANSHUMANISM AND EVOLUTIONARY SPIRITUALITY

Episode 300 — July 10, 2022

CELEBRATING BARBARA MARX HUBBARD: THE ABILITY TO KEEP EVOLVING AND TRANSFORMING

As many of you may know, I was greatly privileged to found *One Mountain* together with my evolutionary partner, Barbara Marx Hubbard. In this 300th week, we were celebrating celebration itself, and what it means to celebrate in the midst of outrageous pain and even existential risk, and why it is essential.

We were celebrating Barbara, and her enormous contribution to evolutionary spirituality.

At the same time, I had read, literally right before that *One Mountain*, a critique (or a number of critiques) of Barbara that very, very seriously criticized particular dimensions of her early expressions of evolutionary spirituality. The critiques that I read were, on the one hand, filled with misinformation, distortion, and alike; however, at the kernel of the critique, there was something that was true and accurate. I was unaware of the specific early quotes—but just in the fragrance of my many conversations with Barbara, when we first met, and first came to create together, **there was a sense of *transhumanist moral neutrality* in relationship to the evolutionary process**, which I found beyond troubling—and shared that with Barbara.

We had a number of fierce contestations and conversations, which were important and wonderful. I was talking about Eros, and Ethos, and *The Universe: A Love story*, or what we also call in CosmoErotic Humanism (which is the name of the new Story of Value we are trying to articulate today in response to existential risk) we also call *Evolution: The Love story of the Universe*, or *the Intimate Universe*, or *the CosmoErotic Universe*, or *the Amorous Cosmos*. The core of this new story is that:

This Amorous Cosmos, this Intimate Universe, lives in us,

- we are expressions of it—and irreducibly unique expressions of it,
- and therefore, every human being has got to be held and honored,
- and the full dignity of the personal can never be bypassed in any evolutionary or transhumanist vision.

Barbara understood that deeply in the context of our conversations, and she did something that people almost never do. She *evolved* her position; she changed her position.

She shared with me that, in her earlier transhumanist days, she had had a very different conception. She used to talk about evolution *not being nice*. Again, although I wasn't familiar with those early writings or citations, Barbara shared with me this earlier sense she had had in transhumanism, which didn't see the centrality of Eros, or what I've called *Unique Self*, or what we refer to, in CosmoErotic Humanism, as *Unique Self Symphony*. **Barbara fully embraced those evolutionary developments as what she**

called *the next step in Conscious Evolution*. That's how she understood our work together.

I have to say that I was blown away by her capacity, in her early, mid, and late 80s:

- To evolve, to transform
- To be fierce in the pursuit of a deeper truth
- To give up being right
- To not hold on
- To have deep regret over earlier positions, that, in the end, turned out to be woefully incomplete

In a word, I have rarely met anyone who had that ability to be constantly evolving herself.

Barbara and I did what we called *Holy of Holies*, which is a phrase that comes from the Jerusalem temple tradition. Holy of Holies is the place where the Ark resided (think *Raiders of the Lost Ark* and Indiana Jones movies). So, the Ark of the Covenant resided in the Holy of Holies, and the **Holy of Holies is a place that is, if you will, safe enough to go all the way in, to think about everything, and to talk about everything.**

Literally, in the last years of Barbara's life, we would do Holy of Holies together, and she would look at every part of her life and see: *what did I get wrong, what did I get right; how can I be better, how can I transform?* It's kind of shocking, and beautiful, and worthy of so much admiration. I am filled with love, and admiration, and honor for Barbara. I am 100% sure that she'd be thrilled with this episode of *One Mountain, Many Paths*.

I also spoke about my colleague, Andrew Cohen before. Andrew, like Barbara, has been very fierce in these past years in evolving and transmuting, and particularly in terms of his thought. In the *One Mountain* broadcast, I shared that I had written a book called *Self*, fiercely critiquing Andrew's evolutionary spirituality position in one particular regard: I critiqued its rejection of the personal, its talk about *the movement beyond yourself as a creative movement that was impersonal*, what Andrew called *the authentic self*, which he described as an awakened *impersonal* function.

This sense of the impersonal as being the penultimate — I found it both structurally invalid, and not in alignment with the realization that the Cosmos is ultimately intimate and personal.

If I can say it this way,

- you *first* have the personal at the level of personality, which is a fragrance of the personal,
- and *then* you clarify, and you step into the impersonal; the realization that you're one with the larger Field.
- But really, that larger Field is not impersonal.

That's one of the ways that I think classical enlightenment teachings misunderstood it. They saw the impersonal as being impersonal in a kind of way that it's not. It is *beyond* personality. It is *beyond* separate self.

That impersonal is the ground of a higher personal. So, if you will, it is—

- personal,
- impersonal,
- then a higher personal beyond the impersonal.

I wrote a book on this called *Self*, which articulated both the vision of Unique Self that appears in the *Unique Self* book, a separate volume, and fiercely critiqued Andrew's position.

Now, I've got to tell you something about Andrew. He received that book with great grace, and great love, and great honor. I spoke about him in that book with honor and love, as a very, very esteemed colleague, who made an enormous contribution to the contemporary articulation of evolutionary spirituality.

Andrew and I viewed this exchange as a kind of *dharma* combat, if you will—but in the most fierce and tender sense of the word. In this particular area, Andrew was very audacious and came very close to my notion of Unique Self. Indeed, he has shared with me, privately and publicly, that he has *evolved* his position, and really incorporated the irreducible uniqueness of the higher individuation *beyond* ego.

I shared a little bit about that *Self* book again as well in this *One Mountain*, which I was glad to do, and I did it, I hope, with great honor for Andrew—and for Barbara—but for Andrew in particular. I am delighted to be engaged with him now in a series of dialogues on evolutionary spirituality, which has been so dear to both Andrew and I for many, many, many years.

We've been privileged to articulate together many of the core tenets in that field that have become almost defaults, in a wonderful way.

We continue to engage from a shared context and a shared space, to try and clarify, and to learn from each other.

That's what we need in conversation.

It is exactly this kind of conversation where we don't *polarize*, where our positions are not about a personal branded identity, but about a deep shared search for the deepest realization.

I think it is a model of where we need to be.

> *The ability to hold paradox together—the paradox of fierce love and occasionally fierce contestation—moves us beyond the polarization.*

That polarization, the way we are unable to have conversations today, is at the core of existential risk.

CELEBRATING 300 WEEKS OF *ONE MOUNTAIN, MANY PATHS*: HUMANS ARE WILDLY GOOD, TRUE AND BEAUTIFUL

Oh, my God!

It's a gorgeous moment. *Celebration!*

- How do we celebrate when the world is so imperfect?
- How do we celebrate when we are poised at this moment, in this time between worlds, in this time between stories?
- When existential risk, and catastrophic risk—which are real—lurk.
- When we realize the system is not too big to fail,
- When unimaginable suffering takes place on the planet and is poised to take place if we don't shift the vector of the human story.

At the same time, utopia lurks—the possibility of creating a world which is unimaginably beautiful, rooted in human dignity—the dignity of every individual, the irreducible dignity of every Unique Self, coming together as Unique Self Symphonies to participate in the true nature of Reality, which is *Evolution: The Love Story of the Universe.*

Not a pollyannish love story—but a story filled with agony and ecstasy, part of a larger field of consciousness, a multi-dimensional field of consciousness, and Reality, and meaning.

Reality is incepted with meaning; it is *suffused* with meaning.

> *Look beside you, and I'm there.*
> *Look behind you, and I am there.*
> *Look above you, and I am there.*
> *Look below you, and I am there.*
> *Look inside you, and I am there.*
> *It is meaning everywhere.*
> *It is value, everywhere.*

One of the principles we established last week is that **you can't change the world unless you're already willing to live in the world that's already changed.**

Do we understand that? What it means is: no matter what's happening, we have to recognize it is not just true that we live in a world of outrageous pain. **We also live in a world of outrageous beauty.**

We live in a world of outrageous pain. That's true. There is no answer. There is no simple theology to answer that question, whether it's a techno-feudalist theology, whether it's a Great Reset theology which argues that human beings are almost implicitly downgraded nanobots, and an upgraded algorithmic web. That kind of theology is absurd, and horrific, and ultimately can lead to very, very great evil. In the same way, certain religious ideologies, which portrayed God in ways that violated the essence of the Divine, also explained away human suffering.

We can never *explain away* human suffering. We have to *respond* to human suffering.

There is no answer to the great question of why Reality is constructed in a way that allows for suffering. We live in a world of outrageous pain.

We cannot answer that question; that question is unanswerable. But we can *respond*; we can respond powerfully and beautifully.

- **We live in a world of outrageous pain,** and the only response to outrageous pain is Outrageous Love.
- At the same time, **we live in a world of outrageous beauty**, everywhere: from colors, to sounds, to the billions of human beings performing random acts of kindness every day, the billions of human beings reaching towards each other, filled with value, and meaning, and kindness, and goodness, and integrity.

The news tracks that which violates the human covenant of goodness. Why? Because that violation is an aberration, it attracts attention, and is reported on the news.

But the true news, the good news, is that *the reason why* it attracts attention is *because* it is a violation of the nature of who and what human beings are.

Human beings are wildly good, and wildly true, and wildly beautiful, and all of that.

We need to be able to find that goodness and articulate the value that lives in us, as us, and through us. We have to know our goodness and create world systems that support and activate that goodness.

Wow! So here we are in Week 300, and we are celebrating! All that was an explanation of *why* we're celebrating. We are celebrating because in order to change the world, you've got to not get bitter, you've got to not get cynical or jaded.

In order to change the world, you have to already be willing to live in the world that's already changed, and the world that's already changed means a world of Goodness, Truth, and Beauty.

- It is a world of celebration, where we celebrate each other, we celebrate life, we celebrate our creativity, we celebrate each other's creativity.
- It is a world in which we're able to apologize and say *I am sorry*.
- It is a world in which in we are able to find, beneath the egoic and angry self, our true nature. Our true nature which is omni-considerate of the whole. Our true nature which desperately wants to embrace and be embraced, which desperately is searching for kindness in all the right places.

So, we are here to celebrate. This is a mad week for massive, wild, and beautiful celebration.

TO GIVE UP BEING RIGHT IS BEING *HOMO AMOR*

Sometimes it is hard.

I just had a phone call with my son, who is a beautiful, beautiful young man, and he is having a hard moment. He kind of clicked off the phone; he said *bye* and clicked off the phone at the end of the conversation. So, I called him back and got mad at him. I said, *Yo, you can't click off the phone that way! You've got to be loving and respectful,* and I got upset. Then I felt terrible for getting upset, and Kristina said I shouldn't have gotten upset, and she was probably right. You feel like, *wow, it's hard.* We are trying to create the most beautiful lovingness in each other.

Then I realized more deeply, in that particular conversation, what my son was trying to say—which I hadn't really heard. He was trying to say something else, and I got it, and some tears went down his cheeks. I said, *Oh, that's what you're saying. I got your back, you're totally right. Got your back, man!* Like, wow, we have to apologize. So, he very sweetly said, *Wow, got it, sorry.* We've got to hang up and say, *love you.* Now I have got to call him back right after Church and say, *You are totally right, but I shouldn't have gotten upset about it.*

There's a thousand interactions like that, in which we've got to:

- Love each other
- Love each other *madly*
- Apologize to each other
- Go deeper with each other
- Protect each other
- **Love it open**

I just want to ask everyone to set the intention of this Week 300, this wild celebration:

If there is anything you are holding, where you feel like you could let go of an egoic attachment, where there's someone you should reach out and say, *wow, I've been holding on to this, I apologize*—do it! I want to go the next step: just literally, right now, **take your phone and call!** Anyone you've refused to reach out to, anyone you've refused to apologize, anyone you've refused to forgive because you are holding on to being right.

*Let's give up being right, all of us, and let's be **Homo amor** right now.*

I want to ask everyone: **if you could reach out, there's a thousand ways to kneel and kiss the ground.**

- Let's do this together, and let's set our intent with an actual action.
- Let's blow open our intention right now.
- Let's reach out right now.

You know what I'm going to do? Hold on one second, let's actually do this.

[*Marc calls his son*]

[*Marc*] *Hey, man! Hey, I'm in the middle of Church right now. I just shared with everyone that you, and I just had a little argument, and I got upset with you. Then I actually thought about it and I realized, although we got to say love each other before we got off the phone, that I shouldn't have gotten that upset about it. So, I am just calling to apologize. Good? Give me your eyes, man. I love you madly, baby!*

[*son*] *But just when you're done, can you call me because I really don't feel comfortable?*

[Marc] I got you, sweetie pie! I'll call you right afterwards. Because I know you want to stay there, and I'll call you right afterwards. Okay, baby? Love you madly.

[son] Yeah, love you!

[Marc] Madly or just regular? No, it might be just regular.

Okay, there we go. Ready, everybody? We are jumping in now. He just wrote: *Love you madly.* Awesome, I'm just writing back, *Love you madly, madly!*

That's our intention, our intention is about *kindness*.

It is about setting the intention for kindness, in a gorgeous and beautiful way, and celebrating. We are going to celebrate this revolution that we are making here.

This revolution we are making here cannot bypass individuals. Barbara Marx Hubbard is my dear evolutionary partner, and the founder, with me, of what we used to call *Evolutionary Church*, we now call *One Mountain, Many Paths*. We are going to listen really deeply to Barbara, and I want to talk about what she says, and how she unpacks it. We are going to listen to Barbara's talk from the very first week of *One Mountain*, of *Evolutionary Church*. We are going to go back to the first week of Evolutionary Church, and we are going to listen to Barbara, which is gorgeous and fantastic. Barbara, in the continuity of consciousness, has never left us and is with us, she is with us more strongly and more beautifully than ever.

We are going to have a very, very serious, sensitive, gorgeous conversation about the shadows of evolutionary spirituality. In other words, **what is the potential shadow of evolutionary spirituality,** that I've talked about for years and that Barbara has talked about for years?

I am going to share with you something very intimate and personal if I can, which is **a very fierce argument that Barbara and I had at the very beginning.** In this case, Barbara thought about it very, very deeply, and she did what I just did with my son and she apologized. Not to me, but she actually said, *I got that wrong.*

There is a particular line of thinking that Barbara got wrong in a very big way. Not just Barbara got it wrong, Teilhard de Chardin got it wrong, Buckminster Fuller, in certain talks he gave, got it wrong.

In general, there is a movement called transhumanism which got something very, very wrong. I've been a major critic of certain dimensions of transhumanism, or evolutionary thought, for many years because of this thing that I think they got wrong, which I think is fundamentally dangerous, and worse than dangerous. It can justify, really, the most tragic parts of humanity.

As we build this revolution, as we look to actually *become* the new human, and to *become* the new humanity, it always has to be rooted in person-to-person kindness.

It's got to be rooted in the immeasurable dignity of every individual—and there's a danger that totalizing systems have…. (That was my son, just texting again, *love madly!*) **There is a danger in totalizing systems that can turn into a kind of eugenics.** Eugenics means:

- You engineer society
- You engineer populations
- You engineer population control

You do this in order to produce the best humanity through a kind of social engineering.

Early transhumanism *believed* in eugenics. **Many people in the scientific community spoke the language of eugenics, and didn't understand the danger.** They also spoke the language of racial inequality, and even people like Teilhard de Chardin spoke that language. Teilhard de Chardin said any number of things that were very clearly eugenics, that were very clearly a kind of social engineering.

Now, that kind of social engineering has been picked up by techno-utopians, people like Mark Zuckerberg. Mark Zuckerberg is a techno-utopian who believes in social engineering. There is an excellent major work published in 2018, out of Cambridge called **Re-Engineering Humanity**[7]. It was published *before* a book that we've talked about often here, which we have both endorsed, *Surveillance Capitalism* by Shoshana Zuboff. So, this 2018 book came out before *Surveillance Capitalism* and **is a very thorough book looking at the dangers of techno-utopia.**

This notion early in transhumanism, in Julian Huxley and Teilhard de Chardin, was picked up in part by Bucky Fuller and by Barbara. Barbara picked this up. There were certain pieces of it that were apparent in Abraham Maslow, and Barbara and I have spent hours talking about this. Abraham Maslow was a key influence on Barbara, as was Bucky Fuller. In many ways, Abraham Maslow and Bucky Fuller did great things, and de Chardin is a very, very important thinker and—they got this wrong, dead wrong!

I articulated the entire vision of Unique Self in response to a number of tragedies in the world system that needed to be corrected, and one of them was **the mystical notion of leaving your separate ego self and becoming True Self, becoming *one with the Field*, which by itself can also lead to totalitarianism. In fact:**

- You don't *just* become one with the Field.
- You don't *just* move beyond your separate self and realize that you are part of a larger Field that is true—that's True Self.
- **But then you need to individuate beyond True Self as an irreducibly unique expression of the Field, which is Unique Self.**

There are two different forms of totalitarianism that emerge from a failure to recognize Unique Self.

---

7   Evan Selinger and Brett Frischmann, *Re-Engineering Humanity* (Cambridge University Press, 2018).

One is a kind of **mystical totalitarianism**, which emerges (and can easily emerge) from certain forms of Eastern mystical thinking, in Buddhism and in other systems.

The second form of totalitarianism is **the totalitarianism of evolutionary spirituality**, in which evolutionary spirituality itself can become this totalizing system that views progress as happening across a kind of linear vector, and then views Reality as ultimately being materialist. Therefore, the human being has to reengineer, or use God as a pantheistic force, but without the sense of the irreducible value of life, and the irreducible value of every individual, the irreducible value of every Unique Self.

That vector, that kind of evolutionary spirituality, can be used to reengineer Reality, and can view social media, for example, as a way to do it.

No one understood the danger of social media when it first began. Everyone was like, *social media was a Godsend*, everyone was a techno-utopian: Everyone was going to have a voice, everyone was going to have a platform and social media was going to be the collective eyes of what de Chardin called the *noosphere*.

But no one understood the danger of social media; that social media was...

- driven by profit vectors
- based on the aggregation of personal data, which then
- micro-targets you
- to undermine your free will—not only to get you to make purchases,
- but to get you to vote in a particular way, and
- to think and feel in a particular way.

So, there was a kind of techno-totalitarian agenda which emerged from the tech plex, which hijacked transhumanism, and particular vectors in transhumanism. That's very, very dangerous.

Barbara and I had a huge fierce argument about this, where Barbara was taking a kind of techno-optimist, but more than optimist, a techno-utopian vision of the human being merging with technology: this new human emerges, and the noosphere is completely merged with technology.

Much of the technological world is going in that direction: augmented reality, virtual reality, avatars, the metaverse, etc. These are all movements in that direction, which have become divorced from what we call here in *One Mountain* and in this new story we're telling: *First Principles and First Values*.

In other words, the tech plex and much of transhumanism has alienated itself from a sense of First Values and First Principles. This is why transhumanism often merges with certain readings of Buddhism. They actually go well together, **but they can become a ground of a worldwide totalitarianism.** So, you have to be very, very careful to repudiate that in no uncertain terms.

At the end of her life, the last five to six years when we were in contact five to six times a day, we had a fierce set of arguments about this which were very beautiful, and Barbara stepped into the part of the new story that I've spent my life on, which is *love*; but love not just as a cosmic force.

> Love as a cosmic force, but not just as a neutral force.
> Love that honors the personal.
> Love that perceives the personal.
> Love that's a perception of the irreducible and infinite dignity of every individual human being.
> Love that demands kindness.
> Love that demands Outrageous Acts of Love.
> Love that's never willing to bypass the dignity of every individual.
> Love that rejects social engineering solutions that are willing to displace and alienate huge sectors of humanity; and not just huge sectors of humanity, but solutions willing to displace and alienate even one human being.

THE EVOLUTION OF LOVE SAYS *NO* TO EUGENICS

This is a very beautiful moment in our celebration week, in this 300th week. We are celebrating the new vision of *Homo amor*. We are celebrating the potential emergence of a new human and a new humanity.

We do that by *being Homo amor*.

- Being *Homo amor* is to be kind.
- Being *Homo amor* is to be fierce, but to be filled with quivering tenderness.
- Being *Homo amor* is to apologize if you got it wrong.
- Being *Homo amor* is to be willing to give up being right, and to stand fiercely for value, to move beyond polarization, and to know that we are together in a Field of Value.

That Field of Value is nurturing, and it is nourishing, and it is loving.

It's a Field of Value in which no one is left out of the circle. It's a Field the Value that rejects *in toto*, as a moral abhorrence, the kind of positions like eugenics that de Chardin and many other extremely respectable figures endorsed. It was considered a *genuine possibility* in the most respectable of circles!

Evolution of love says no to eugenics.

The evolution of love says *no* to transhumanist possibilities that become dystopian, because they become the ground of totalitarianism. This is a very important thing to do, in Week 300.

It is important to be very, very careful that there are certain trends out there that you hear a lot about, which bring together a kind of Buddhist *no-self*, in which enlightenment is moving beyond the self, and being in the field of *no-self* where the personal is lost, which rejects the personal.

They then merge it together with evolutionary spirituality, the sense of evolution, and the transhumanist materialist trends which fail to honor the irreducible dignity of every individual, which talk about things like culling the herd, and become a kind of Thanos.

Remember Thanos? Right before COVID, in 2017–2019, Marvel Studios put out two movies called *The Avengers*, in which the world is faced with existential risk and the villain is Thanos.

Thanos is essentially a transhumanist.

Thanos is an evolutionary spirituality person, and a Buddhist. But when I say "Buddhist," I mean he's a surface vision of Buddhism. It is not the depth of Buddhism, but it's the surface vision of distorted Buddhism, which says that no-self is the end of the story.

Thanos decides that the only way to save humanity is to *cull the herd*, and to kill half of humanity. The Avengers don't even know how to tell him that he's wrong; they don't know how to explain that he got it wrong, they don't know how to do that. Thanos is much more elegant and eloquent.

In the second movie, we see Thanos, as the sun rises, meditating, contemplating, eating out of a rice bowl, being a good crunchy. A good crunchy, meaning: a good techno-optimist, techno-utopian hippie, eating crunchy and meditating after he killed half of the world.

This is a very big deal! That's exactly what we reject here!

We need to integrate the best of the premodern, modern, and postmodern era. How often have we said that? A thousand times! This means:

- **We need to integrate the best interior science of the great traditions**, which speak of the potential for human dignity, which is the innate value of every human being.
- We need to integrate the best of **modernity**, which moves *beyond the ethnocentric limitation* of that human dignity that the traditions imposed, when the traditions said, *it's only my people who have value, only my people have dignity*. Modernity moved into a universal set of human rights, a sense of uni-

versal dignity of men, and moved then into postmodernity.

- We need to integrate the best of **postmodernity,** which was then about not just men but women, and not just landowners, but every human being, and all those who are marginalized: all of the LGBT communities, and all of the trans communities, and all of the marginalized communities that have been actually alienated because they don't fit into the way we think that people should think, or live, or play, or sex. Everyone has a seat at the table; there's no one who's left out of the circle. That's postmodernity's advance into value, which is wildly important. It's an evolution of love.

As we articulate *Homo amor*, we have to articulate the best of premodern traditional value, the best of modern value, the best of postmodern insight and value and synergize that into what we call a new *evolving perennialism* integrating the perennial truths from all of the different moments in history, across space and time, into a new story that we can tell in five minutes anywhere and everywhere. In this new story every human being understands that I am part of The Universe: A Love story; that evolution is the Love story of the Universe; and that evolution is evolving. Evolving is the evolution of love, meaning that we move from egocentric love to ethnocentric love, in the premodern period, to worldcentric love (every human being), to cosmocentric love (every animal).

No one is left outside the circle. We care about every human being.

Our experience of intimacy, care, and concern is for every living being, every human being, and for the planet itself. That's what we're going for!

THE TECHNO-UTOPIAN VISION NEEDS TO BE GROUNDED IN UNIQUE SELF

In this moment, I want to just bring to the table, specifically in this moment of celebration, the shadows of evolutionary spirituality, and really honor Barbara Marx Hubbard, because **Barbara was always willing to evolve, she never freeze-framed.**

When we started studying together, we did Holy of Holies, which is our context; it's a term from the temple in Jerusalem, *Sanctum Sanctorum*, which is part of my lineage tradition. In the temple tradition of Jerusalem, the inner sanctum was called Holy of Holies. So, when I do study sessions, we call them Holy of Holies. Barbara and I did these study sessions for five years, almost once a week, and we studied these issues very, very deeply.

Of course, I madly enjoyed the depth of our study, and Barbara came to the conclusion, and I think she was correct, that transhumanism made huge mistakes, and that some of her expressions were transhumanist expressions. Some of them had been taken out of context, but there were core transhumanist expressions that Barbara articulated here and there that were in the tradition of Bucky Fuller and de Chardin that were wrong, and that were dead wrong.

She realized that the techno-utopian visio:

- Needed to be grounded in Unique Self
- Needed to be grounded in intrinsic value
- Needed to be grounded in evolutionary love that honors the dignity of every individual

She spent the last five to six years of her life—after recounting and rejecting the weaknesses of those early transhumanist views—trying to articulate this new vision of *Homo amor*. Every once in a while, she'd slip into a techno-utopian moment, which talked about the good of social media without seeing its weakness.

Social media has a lot of good, but it has enormous addictive and dehumanizing weakness, and it's also the ground for information warfare, which is warping our body politic, and warping our ability to create The Universe: A Love story. She would sometimes slip back into a kind of idealization of social media as *the eyes of the noosphere*, and sometimes that would even happen here in *One Mountain*. Then I would either object on the spot, or we'd talk about it afterwards and we'd reformulate it the next week.

I want to really hold something very deeply, and I want to also model something else:

It would be very easy to take certain quotes of Barbara's, string them together, and then to demonize her. But of course, that would be the same expression of un-love. Barbara is not here to articulate her evolved position. She articulated it to me, many, many, many, many times, over hundreds of hours of conversation. It was very clear to me. It's easy to attack Barbara, to identify her with the de Chardin and Bucky Fuller lineage, which was a beautiful lineage, but which had certain articulations which came close to—or were—certain forms of eugenics that were acceptable at the time, but actually were dead wrong.

Now, again, **we have to allow a person to make a tragic mistake** when the times move in that direction, no matter how wrong the mistake is, **we have to embrace the fullness of who they are**, and **we have to reject their position if they had a position that was wrong** and embrace the full goodness of who they are.

Barbara Marx Hubbard was an unbelievably good person, an unbelievably kind person, who had a deep vision of the goodness of humanity. She dedicated her life, day and night, to addressing the profound suffering on the planet, and to articulating a new vision. I am proud to stand with her as her evolutionary partner, proud that she is the co-founder of *One Mountain, Many Paths*, and proud of her for doing that very, very difficult thing that people rarely do, which is to say: *Oh, my God, I made a horrible mistake in one dimension of my thought, and I'm going to correct it the best I can.*

The way that she did that was to embrace the notion of the irreducible Unique Self of the individual, of the irreducible rights of every individual, and to reject that early transhumanist division. This is a very big deal, my friends!

Now with that, I am madly delighted. Barbara, it's a great pleasure, a great honor, to be your friend and your evolutionary partner. I admire you not only for your brilliance, depth, and creativity, but for your courage to recognize the things you got wrong, like we all get things wrong.

The more significant the thinker, the more you can get something wrong. I'm sure that de Chardin and Bucky Fuller, if they had seen the ways that some of their articulations could have been distorted, they would have recanted them also, as we should. That's a big deal.

So, knowing and recognizing the potential shadows of evolutionary spirituality is unbelievably important, and that's why evolutionary spirituality, while being enormously important, is not our banner. I think everyone here knows, our banner, what we call the new story, is CosmoErotic Humanism. CosmoErotic meaning, **Eros is the quality of Cosmos that lives and suffuses all of Reality**. As in the Song of Solomon, *its insides are lined with love.*

But hear the next sentence:

CosmoErotic Humanism means: the irreducible dignity of every individual, standing for kindness, for goodness, for truth and for beauty in every individuated human form.

It's CosmoErotic Humanism.

From the place of that humanism, we move from egocentric love, to ethnocentric love, to worldcentric love, to cosmocentric love, where I realize:

- I am Evolutionary Love,
- I am an irreducibly unique expression of the evolutionary Eros,
- I am omni-considerate for the sake of the whole.

We come together in Unique Self Symphony in which every human being plays their unique instrument, and *the hills become alive with the sound of love and the sound of music*[8].

EVOLUTIONARY LOVE CODE: MOVING BEYOND DEMONIZATION

That which unites us is far greater than that which divides us.

We are united in a shared story of value.

That does not make us perfect expressions of that value. We are all imperfect vessels for the light; the imperfect vessels for the holy and broken *Hallelujahs*.

We must move beyond demonization, to daemon-isation.

It is only the loss of daemon that turns us into demon.

When we are not inside the circle together, we place others outside the circle as a way of pretending that we are on the inside.

Only a shared story based on First Principles and First Values serves as the ground for a global ethos for a global civilization.

That's *One Mountain*. That is who we are. That's our credo.

INCARNATING THE IMPULSE OF EVOLUTION: BARBARA'S FIRST SERMON IN *EVOLUTIONARY CHURCH*

The intention for Evolutionary Church, the inner impulse in you, that is activating you to experience this prayer, to experience this evolution, is a frequency. It comes from the source of creation that has been evolving for billions and billions of years—in each one of us. **We are each uniquely coded with the frequency of the entire evolutionary journey that**

---

8   Alluding to musical drama film: "The Sound of Music," 1965, and the song "The hills are alive"

is wanting to come forward now as our own expressions of love, of creativity, of vocation. Each of us is literally coded with the evolutionary impulse of creation.

So, the intention of the *Evolutionary Church* is to create:

- A field for the evolution of humanity
- A space in consciousness
- A space in being with one another where this profound evolutionary impulse in each one of us comes to consciousness
- A space where it gives us guidance through that impulse, as to our *own unique gift to the world*; as to *our own unique voice* that Marc calls Unique Self Symphony

Just imagine for a moment, every voice on this planet impelled by the impulse of creation, uniquely in each person sounding the note of inspiration, of creativity, of desire to give your gift to the whole sounding as **Unique Self -Symphony**. How does that symphony express itself?

The vision is for the Evolutionary Church expressing itself in a *planetary awakening in love*. It expresses itself in a birth of humanity capable of co-evolving with nature, co-creating with Spirit. It awakens in a humanity capable of using our spiritual, social, scientific, technological genius.

We restore the Earth to free the people, to explore the vast regions of inner space and the cosmos beyond this planet. The intention of the *Evolutionary Church* is to be a birthing place for the co-evolution of humanity.

How is this going to happen?

One of the key ways and one of the key practices, as Marc mentioned, is *prayer*. **Another practice is the incarnation of the impulse of evolution, holding yourself in conscious awareness.**

I'd like to carry you through this for one moment. I think of it as an...

EVOLUTIONARY CHAKRA MEDITATION

First, put your mind in the mind of God at the origin of creation.

Imagine that eternal process becoming coded through that Big Bang and going through the billions of years of evolution. Genius creating life, human life, and now your own life as an impulse of those billions of years. We're sitting right at the edge of the billions of years.

Now bring it right in your base chakra and feel there the security of the entire impulse of creation, indwelling as you, as your security, the invisible force within us.

Now bring that billions of years from the mind of God right up through your base chakra into your generative organs.

Feel yourself shifting from devolution towards evolution, from degeneration toward regeneration.

Feel yourselves being activated, "Oh, there's more for us to do, there's more for us to be." We are now expressing this process of creation, uphold that impulse once again, breathe it out all the way through the base chakra to the generative organs, and take it into the power center.

As we enter the Evolutionary Church, the power of the process of creation is in every one of us, uniquely expressing as our own impulse to give, to be, to reach out. Feel the enormity of that power in you. You recognize it's coming from the source of creation, uniquely, as you.

Take in one more deep breath up through all the chakras through the base chakra to the generative organs. You are regenerating the Evolutionary Church; you are expressing your full power.

Bring it right up into the place where the emotions dwell, the pain, the sorrow, the separation, the feeling of inadequacy; that place where you say "I'm not good enough, I'll never make it. It won't be me. Where am I going? I don't know what to do."

Let that impulse, which has direction, which has purpose, which has the knowledge of creation within it, let it go through those emotions. Let it organize and calibrate those emotions into a field in which they go directly into the heart.

All of our emotions, whatever feelings of separation we may have had, let it go into the heart. And in that heart of unconditional love, we find the basic impulse of evolution. The Evolutionary Church sets the intention to bring forth the impulse of Eros in evolution into the heart of all our members, of all of humanity. Just feel that in your heart, feel the almost infinite expression of Love.

Let it out the whole way, don't hold any of it back. In the Evolutionary Church, we do not need to hold our love of one another back. Let that evolution in your heart go right up into your upper heart, which is your vocation. Your gift of love to the world, your unique expression, your vocation of destiny, what the impulse of evolution is born in you to do.

In the Evolutionary Church it is our intention to bring forth that intention of creation in each of us. Let it be not just a personal, separate intention or project. Let it be within us a unique expression of the genius of evolution as our own calling, our own vocation. Let us incarnate the genius of evolution in our expressions in the world. As we share our vocations with each other in this Church and learn to connect our vocations with one another as expressions of the divine impulse of creation, let us feel the glory of the empowerment of all of humanity wherever we congregate in the community. Let us feel it in the communion of the evolutionary potential, which is nurtured in this Church.

Take in one more deep breath, everybody together, one deep breath from the source of creation all the way up through the genius of evolution, through the lower chakras, through the heart, through the vocation of destiny.

Now, bring it into your voice. When you have a chance to speak later on in this Church, let your voice be the frequency of the impulse of evolution within you. That voice is different from the purely mental mind. It is the voice that holds the quality, the resonance, the frequency of that impulse as you. When you speak it through the planetary symphony, the Unique Self Symphony, when you speak it into the noosphere or the thinking layer of earth or social media or the internet, you are expressing the voice of creation, as you, into the field, through a Unique Self Symphony.

Then let it go all the way on up into your third eye now, to the spiritual awakening of almost infinite intelligence pulsing through each one of us. Let us bring it up, bring it down, bring it in and bring it out.

Recognize that this is the intention of Evolutionary Church: to nurture the incarnation of the evolutionary impulse in each one of us as conscious evolutionaries; as beings born at the precise moment when evolution becomes conscious of itself in others, when evolution becomes aware of itself as evolution by choice, by prayer, by intention, by inspiration, by creation, by joining together in Love. It is the intention of the Evolutionary Church to offer a new sacred space in the world for people to gather, to evolve in love and give their unique gift to our Unique Self Symphony for a planetary awakening.

Let me just finish with the thought of the birth of a co-creative humanity as a planetary awakening in love. It is like the birth of a newborn child when its nervous system just barely links up. It opens its eyes and, if it's very fortunate, it is held in the arms of its mother. The baby is placed in the mother's arms against the mother's heart. The baby feels the heartbeat from that mother awakening its nervous system to the realization that it is loved. **The intention of the Evolutionary Church is to generate the awareness that we are loved. That we are created by a universal process of creation that has direction, has purpose, has intention. Its intention is higher consciousness, greater freedom, more complex and loving order.**

Every impulse in every one of us toward consciousness, freedom, and love is being impelled in the Evolutionary Church, in the Unique Self Symphony, toward a planetary awakening to literally help the world shift from a phase of devolution and crisis to a phase of evolution and co-creation.

- *Everyone* is precious.
- *Every* voice is needed.
- *Every one* of us is orchestrated by the invisible process of creation coming to a new climax in the evolutionary planetary awakening in love, in our lifetime.

So here we are gathered for the very first time in this new space expressing a global communion of pioneering souls, worldwide.

LEAVING THE PERSONAL BEHIND LEADS TO TOTALITARIANISM

Now, I [Marc] want to just share something with you, and this is a very intimate moment between us at *One Mountain*. Notice that at this point, Barbara and I had spoken at length. Of course, in the first week, when Barbara finished, I then did part two. But Barbara, already in this talk, was doing something well beyond the early shadows of transhumanism and evolutionary spirituality. At this point, she had *integrated* all our conversations about Unique Self, and our terms:

- Unique Self Symphony, a term that Barbara and I coined together:
- A Planetary Awakening in Love through Unique Self Symphonies.

That phrase is a precise critique of the earlier transhumanist vision, and an expression of this shared vision of this new emergent evolutionary spirituality, which is of an entirely different quality and order. We hadn't even coined the term *CosmoErotic Humanism* yet.

But what's critical is to understand is that **Unique Self is at the core.**

Unique Self is the unique expression of the evolutionary impulse awake and alive in me.

What Barbara was doing in that meditation in the first week of One Mountain, the evolutionary chakra meditation, was a direct experience of all of the evolutionary spiral, all of the evolutionary impulse from matter to life to mind, literally, awake and alive in me.

That's critical. Without that, I don't know who I am. **The embrace of my evolutionary self is essential to my identity.** Yet, that evolutionary self is not just *an authentic self.*

I wrote a book which I was very privileged to write, it's a book called *Self*, critiquing my colleague, Andrew Cohen, who was expressing a vision of *authentic self* beyond the personal.

I was quite convinced, and remain convinced, that that vision could actually create totalitarianism, that the transhumanist vision merged with Eastern mysticism could lead to totalitarianism. Because in Andrew's vision of the authentic self, he describes the authentic self as an awakened *impersonal* function. Meaning:

- the personal is left behind at **separate self,**
- and, in Andrew's vision at the time, you then move beyond from separate self to **True Self**, to the realization of Eastern mysticism and Western mysticism that *I am one with the Field.*
- Then, Andrew talked about then moving beyond True Self to **authentic self, which is this impersonal, evolutionary impulse creatively moving in me.**

I said to Andrew, as I said to Barbara, *Andrew, that will yield totalitarianism.*

You never leave the personal behind, ever! **Any system that argues that we leave the personal behind will at some point become totalitarian.** That's critical to understand.

Again, I want to really honor Andrew, because Andrew has completely shifted his position, and in any number of private conversations with me and in public dialogues that we've done, he has transmuted his position, and realized that you cannot talk about authentic self without understanding the irreducible uniqueness and irreducible dignity of every individual—that is, without embracing what I call *the personal beyond the impersonal.*

Any position that doesn't recognize the irreducible dignity of the personal has no place.

The early evolutionary spirituality positions, as articulated by Barbara (which came out of Teilhard de Chardin's and Bucky Fuller's transhumanism), and as articulated by Andrew and evolutionary spirituality, had enormous good in them, but also had this enormous shadow which needed to be recognized.

There is a way that we can hold each other in our beauty, *and* **call each other to our best, to our deepest. It's not to demonize, but to find what's beautiful, and then to transmute, to transform, and to allow people to transform.** So, if someone has a position which is actually flawed, and it can lead to terrible consequences, we need to critique that position, whether that's the position of the Jesuits in the Catholic Church, whether it's positions within Islam, whether it's positions within Christianity or within Judaism, or whether it's positions within worlds of evolutionary spirituality.

We need to create a new story which is going to generate the most good for the most people, and for most of life, and then for all of life, and for all people.

In other words, we have to:

- Go from a very, very small sector of the people who are included in our love, which is **ethnocentric love**
- Explode that boundary into **worldcentric love**: every human being
- Expand it to **all of the Living Universe**
- Ultimately, expand it to **the Universe itself**

We need to be engaged in the evolution of love, and we need to not freeze-frame people on their mistakes. If a leader makes a mistake, whether personally or in terms of their position and their worldview, they get to sincerely transform their position, and everyone needs to do that.

In terms of the transhumanist position, not only Barbara but most of the leaders of what is identified today as the evolutionary community, made some version of this mistake. **That mistake congealed their confluence with the techno-utopian position that was emerging out of Silicon Valley, which itself had emerged from hijacking the materialist and pantheistic versions of transhumanism, which devalue the personal.**

All of those were fiercely fundamental mistakes, which in this week of celebration—it's why I chose this week—need to be corrected. We have rejected all those positions in the very core of CosmoErotic Humanism and articulated this vision of Unique Self and Unique Self Symphony.

Again, I want to say this one more time, because there's no greater praise I could give to a person. Barbara fiercely examined her own positions, evolved them, regretted, and actually had deep remorse, and changed her position in the most fundamental of ways. I am beyond impressed. **I have rarely, almost never, seen a thinker with that kind of courage, with that kind of fierce intellectual integrity.**

STORY AS PRAYER: AUTHENTIC MYSTICAL ECSTASY NEVER IGNORES THE HUNGER OF EVEN ONE INDIVIDUAL

In the first week, where Barbara gave her first evolutionary sermon, in my evolutionary sermon that week—we now call them *evolutionary sensemakings*—I talked about prayer. We pray not to the god you don't believe in—*the god you don't believe in doesn't exist*—but **we pray to the Infinity of Intimacy, the personal force of Cosmos, that not only lives in us, but holds us.**

I want to finish today, instead of prayer, with a story. In many of the great traditions, particularly in the Hebrew lineage, sometimes, when prayer wasn't enough, they would tell a story, and **telling the story is considered prayer.** So, I want to express our prayer in this story, which I think captures everything.

Of course, if I can say, it is not by accident that today began with a little bit of a broken heartedness. I got on the phone a little bit brokenhearted, because I felt I didn't find my son in the right way. And so all of us went to find people, and apologize, just for a little moment, just *a little nothing moment.*

But those *nothing* moments are everything. **There is no moment that's a *nothing* moment.** These moments *matter!*

So I want to tell you a story that captures this, and we will end with this story. This story is a story as prayer.

> Levi Isaac of Berditchev is this great non-dual Hasidic master, and I would say, of all stories, this is my favorite story. He is this great Hasidic master and a great evolutionary thinker when you read him carefully. My academic mentor at Oxford University, Moshe Idel, has written in a book called *Absorbing Perfections* a very, very important work on Levi Isaac.

Levi Isaac is **a great non-dual realizer**, meaning he has an enormous sense of True Self, of being one with the Field of Consciousness, and he also has an enormous sense of the unique individual. He had a beautiful voice.

Once a year in the Hebrew lineage tradition, there is a day called Yom Kippur. It is an amazing day of practice, in which, in the inner lineage, all the gates are opened. **It is a day when we can not only change the vector of a personal life but actually change the vector of history.**

Levi Isaac used to lead the prayer services on Yom Kippur, with the power of his voice, and the power of his prayer, and the power of what they call *Yichudim*: mystical unifications which try and reweave history, and try and evolve history, and end suffering.

In this particular year, he was leading the prayer services, and his voice was strong, and his intention was pure, and his heart was wide open, and his capacity to concentrate and weave together these *Yichudim*, these mystical unions or unifications of world, was at the highest capacity of his life. **He was ascending, they say, to all of the highest spheres, the highest heavens.**

I've got to tell you one other thing: Yom Kippur is a fast day, and the fast goes for about 25 hours. By the very end of the fast day, it was like the end of the 24 hours, Levi Isaac was so high, and the power of his voice, and the power of the purity of his intention, and the power of his mystical capacity, and the power of his *Yichudim* was so potent and so intense that he literally was storming heaven.

He was literally about to accomplish the great evolutionary mission to climax history in a great utopia, which would then suffuse historical Reality. He was the most powerful evolutionary spiritual thinker, who was now at this ultimate moment of evolutionary mystical activism, about to change all of history; the ultimate transhumanist, about to heal all human suffering.

Then, as he was just about to break through—and we are now in the 25th hour of the fast, so people are hungry—somehow, as he is in this mystical ecstasy, he becomes aware of this old man sitting near him in the study hall, who's hungry. He is hungry, and he's about to pass out.

An authentic mystical ecstasy never ignores hunger; it never ignores the hunger of even one individual. So, as Levi Isaac is about to break through in this great evolutionary transhumanist moment, about to invoke the end of history and the new human and the new humanity, as he feels—intruding on his mystical ecstasy—the hunger of but *one old man*, he immediately stops his evolutionary spiritual activism.

He descends from the highest heavens immediately, he ends the fast, and he goes himself to pour a glass of water, and to bring a glass of water to this old man.

That's *Homo amor*! That's who we are. That's who we have to be.

Wow, mad celebration of Barbara Marx Hubbard!

Mad celebration of 300 weeks of this great place of revolution, where we are committed to telling the new Story of Value, and to invoking the new human and new humanity.

The story! We've got to get it right!

This is the place where we refine the story, so that it can be told from every rooftop, so the trumpets can blow, and **we can respond to outrageous pain with the greatest act of Outrageous Love of this generation, which is to tell the new Story of Value**.

To articulate a universal grammar of value that invokes the triumph of the egocentric or ethnocentric *Homo sapiens* into *Homo amor*. Which invokes the beauty, the kindness, the integrity, the wonder, the beauty of the new human and the new humanity.

CHAPTER FIVE

CELEBRATING THE COURAGE TO EVOLVE: BEYOND THE DARK SHADOWS OF TRANSHUMANISM AND EVOLUTIONARY SPIRITUALITY, PART 2

Episode 301 — July 17, 2022

JOINING OF GENIUS

Welcome, everyone, and welcome Barbara Marx Hubbard, my evolutionary partner who I am filled with honor and respect for, and from whom I learned so much, and was just so delighted to share so much.

What Barbara and I engaged in—and this is what really founded this space, and we're all engaging it together in a larger field—is in what we called **not the joining of genes, but the joining of genius.**

Now, that's not my phrase, that's Barbara's phrase, and Barbara was audacious in this phrase. So, of course I'm not claiming for myself Barbara's genius, but I'm going to use that phrase anyway.

In other words, what she was pointing towards is this notion of *genius* joining. In the language that I have used it's called *The Future of Relationships: From Role mate,* to Soul mate, to Whole mate. Whole mate is that next level, which is not joining genes, it's joining genius for the sake of the whole. That's a new level of relationship.

THE SECOND SHOCK OF EXISTENCE: THE DEATH OF OUR HUMANITY

We have a huge summer coming up. I mean, we're doing our 10th annual intensive Mystery School in response to existential risk and in response to catastrophic risk, in response to a world that's filled with outrageous pain and outrageous beauty, realizing that for the first time in human history, we could have no future.

We're standing in this moment, what Robert J. Lifton, the eminent scholar, calls "facing apocalypse," meaning we refuse to turn away.

We actually take into our very being, the experience of there being no future. Not in a way which shatters us, but in a way which enlivens us, and calls us to be the voice of the future in the Now, to do everything in our power as evolution moves in us to change the vector of history.

We change the vector of history by telling a new story.

That's what happened in the Renaissance as the premodern period was breaking down and the Black Death swept Europe. The Renaissance was indeed a time between worlds and a time between stories.

What have we been doing at the Center in all those years? We've been engaged in this response to existential risk, to what we began calling in 2011 *the second shock of existence*.

The first shock of existence is the experience of the human being, not the *biological* experience, but the *existential* experience of death. The experience that death actually *lurks*, and that a life ends: that while there's continuity of consciousness there's also, not as a bug, but as a feature in the system, an experience of death. That's shocking. That's *the first shock of existence*: the death of the human being.

We began talking about *the second shock of existence* in 2011 after I gave a series of talks at Venwoude, where Chahat and her partner, Ted, organized a community for 30 to 40 years.

The second shock of existence is the experience not of the death of the individual human being, but of the potential death of humanity.

The general response to that is *to look away*. I started saying about a decade ago that the systems will break down and fail because such is the structure and the source code. Not the surface. On the desktop, it all looks fine.

But if you go into the source code, the civilizational source code, you actually realize that:

> *The source code itself is broken in certain key segments of the source code text.*

If we don't actually evolve the source code, if we don't engage in what we do here at One Mountain in *evolutionary sensemaking*, or what we might also call *source code conversations*, meaning not just conversations of the mind but also conversations of the body, conversations of the heart, embodied conversations, if we don't engage in source code conversations, if we don't do evolutionary sensemaking that leads to an evolution of the source code, then the vector of the distorted plotline of Reality—the distortion of intentional and inherent plotlines of Reality that have been hijacked by evolution that has stalled—points toward dystopia.

There's this huge gap between interior technologies and exterior technologies. When evolution stalls, exterior technologies exponentialize, weaponized exterior technologies exponentialize with the capacity to destroy humanity, we are facing existential risk not through a nuclear bomb that requires state power to enact it, but actually through any number of forms of organized destruction through various kinds of weaponized systems, which present *certain forms* of existential risk, or the kind of existential risk which is not about the death of humanity but the death of *our* humanity.

There are two forms of existential risk: the death of humanity, and the death of *our* humanity.

CONSCIOUS EVOLUTION AND THE WHEEL OF CO-CREATION

We've been talking about that for quite a few years here, and we've been working to actually do the *one ninja move*, the gorgeous, beautiful, sacred imperative of our time, which is actually to rewrite the source code.

- That's what da Vinci and his cohorts did in the Renaissance. Marsilio Ficino, and the whole gang of the Renaissance, which, as we've pointed out time and again, didn't have more than a thousand people in it.
- There was this inner group of people who came together and said, *we're going to actually rewrite the source code*, we're going to participate in the evolution of love, we're ready to play a larger game and to participate in the evolution of love.

Barbara Marx Hubbard played a key role in articulating particular dimensions, particularly in championing an idea—developed by Julian Huxley that actually appears already in a number of places in interior sciences, that Charles Sanders Pierce articulated in a very beautiful way in an essay—called *Evolutionary Love*.

Barbara picked up not on the **Evolutionary Love** side; that's really where I spend my time and energy. Barbara picked up on the notion of **conscious**

evolution and really shared that idea very powerfully in the world for decades.

She shared that idea in organized networks and SynCons, in conversations and conferences to organize synergistic convergence, as what Barbara called *The Wheel of Co-Creation* to connect what's working worldwide, to advocate for a kind of social synergy, to locate what's working worldwide already in all the sectors of civilization.

Incredibly important!

Then Barbara and I came together and we rewrote *The Wheel of Co-Creation*, and we called it *The Wheel of Co-Creation 2.0*.

1. The rewriting of that Wheel was in order to address certain key pieces that were missing in the initial explosion of beauty and creativity which Barbara did, which was Wheel 1.0. That's number one.
2. But number two, it was to address certain essential broken parts of the source code that were part of the early transhumanist movement, which were part of the early Evolutionary Spirituality movement that inspired Barbara, and she both adopted and contributed to it in enormous ways.

I hope that we modeled how we have a conversation with mad love and honor for Barbara and who she was, and her goodness, and her contribution and the depth of it. I'm sure, there's no one who was more ecstatic at last week's One Mountain than Barbara.

THE SHADOW OF EVOLUTIONARY SPIRITUALITY AND TRANSHUMANISM

So, what prompted the conversation last week was a series of public critiques of Barbara, which had two kinds of information. Let me say it a little more clearly.

THE NEXT STEP IN CONSCIOUS EVOLUTION

One kind of information was just distorted and false.

It characterized, for example, institutions like *HeartMath* as participating in some global conspiracy to oppress the masses and lure them into a kind of torporific slumber, into a kind of docile sleep, so that the agents of the *Great Reset* could take over. That, of course, has nothing to do with what HeartMath is. HeartMath is an excellent institution.

I had one set of extensive conversations with one party who was a key figure there, but I've never been associated with them. Quite a few of my friends were in different places. They've done fantastic and beautiful work, and they have nothing to do with how they were described, for example, in one of those posts critiquing Barbara.

In other words, there's an enormous amount of information in those posts that are linked together to create a conspiratorial thread, when in fact, it's simply not true. It simply doesn't characterize the truth in any sense, shape, or form. That's number one.

But number two, there was in those conversations, a thread of quotations from Barbara, and from de Chardin, and from Buckminster Fuller, but particularly from Barbara, which were chilling.

Now, I don't have my library with me at the moment. Barbara left me when she passed, all of her books. But I don't have my library with me, so I haven't been able to check the context of the quotes. But the quotes in and of themselves were chilling. They talked about what I would call a kind of *Thanos possibility*.

What I mean by a Thanos possibility is, if I can hark back to a public culture text: *The Avengers* out of Marvel Studios, which in 2018 and 2019 described a world facing existential risk. The League of superheroes, *The Avengers*, don't know what to do. There's one person who faces the apocalypse by the name Thanos. Thanos is both the villain and the hero of the story:

- **He's the villain** because he makes a decision to in one instant,

painlessly, wipe out half of humanity in order to save the other half, which is a shocking and a reprehensible moral decision for many, many, many reasons. Because Thanos had actually made the decision that this was the only thing to do. He felt that no one else had the courage to look directly at the apocalypse and make the hard decision.
- However, if you notice when you watch the movie, **Thanos is not your classical villain**. Thanos is not your classical villain in any way. We see Thanos as this much more complex figure, and that's how he was painted by Marvel Studios, making these hard decisions.
- Thanos' own home planet is destroyed because the leadership of Thanos' planet refuses to directly face existential risk, and so everyone dies of starvation. Thanos grows up with that trauma, and he commits himself not to allow that trauma to be repeated on a galactic level.

Now, it's not by accident that this is the scene in popular culture in 2018 and 2019, right before COVID. Of course, the reviewers of *The Avenger* movies kind of missed this. Or they characterize Thanos as a villain and didn't understand the complexity of the Thanos character; and if we were doing an analysis of that movie, I would walk through five or six scenes where Thanos appears as a transhumanist. He appears as an early transhumanist who's committed to some form of eugenics, some form of population control, in order to save humanity from itself. So again, Thanos is this very complex figure.

In the opening of the second Avengers movie, we see him barefoot in his little cabin. He didn't go live in a palace after he destroyed half of the world. He lives in a little cabin. He's eating a rice bowl, probably from some good San Francisco restaurant, kind of completely healthy, i.e. tuna poke bowl maybe. He's watching the sunset and he's meditating. So, he has this transhumanist cast to him. He's saving the world, but he's making decisions that, from an ordinary perspective, seem morally reprehensible. In fact, they *are* morally reprehensible.

The problem is that the Avengers, who all challenged him, don't know how to articulate what's wrong with what he did. Why is he wrong? Why is Thanos wrong?

So when the Avengers, try to confront Thanos, Thanos speaks with great articulation and clarity and moral purpose and passion. The Avengers are filled with passion, but have no moral clarity. They know he's wrong, and they're right that he's wrong. To be clear, Thanos is wrong.

There are dark, shadow versions of both evolutionary spirituality and of transhumanism.

It's those shadow versions that Barbara, in her early days, apparently echoed. I caught fragrances of this when Barbara and I spoke, and we had fierce arguments. Barbara went through a great evolutionary transformation and shifted her position, and merged, if you will, as Barbara and I went through our process of being evolutionary partners and *evolutionary whole mates*, meaning we were working together for the sake of the whole; we were not joining *genes*, but joining *genius*.

She went through a process of actually abandoning those early positions.

But I myself wasn't even aware of the full weight of them until I researched and looked up some of the citations that appeared in a number of these conversations, and they are chilling. They are citations from Teilhard de Chardin that are chilling. But that was the nature of the conversation then, and that's very important to understand.

In mainstream society, there was a mainstream moral society conversation about eugenics, about certain transhumanist possibilities.

That's a big deal. There was an inability then in society to challenge them. In the end, they got challenged because we realized that they lead to things like Nazism. Nazism actually cited early eugenics as a justification.

> *Nazism is and was a shadow form, an extreme shadow form, of evolutionary spirituality.*

That's absolutely true.

Of course, Yuval Harari in his book *Homo Deus* is not incorrect, as a historian, in characterizing some of the most grotesque movements in human history, particularly in their transhumanist 19th and 20th century forms, as distorted formulations of Evolutionary Spirituality. Now, Harari doesn't exactly present them as distorted formulations. He just presents them as formulations of Evolutionary Spirituality, but they're *distorted* formulations. They are dark shadows of Evolutionary Spirituality and Transhumanism that we need to evolve beyond.

But Evolutionary Spirituality itself is enormously important, and a cogent version of Evolutionary Spirituality is enormously important.

So, we need to actually radically reject the dark shadow, which is the Thanos option. The Avengers want to do that in that *Avengers* movie, but they don't quite know how to do it.

Why? **Because they're lacking** *a grammar of value* **which can adequately and potently and compellingly challenge Thanos.**

Because *The Avengers* are emergent from Marvel Studios, and Marvel Studios is a postmodern expression of media culture, which is afraid to claim objective value and intrinsic value, which is afraid to claim what we call *First Principles and First Values embedded in a Story of Value.*

> *When you don't have First Principles and First Values embedded in the Story of Value, you actually don't know how to challenge Thanos.*

In other words, the scriptwriters of Marvel Studios, making *The Avengers* movies, know Thanos is wrong; they can feel it in their bodies. Yet they paint Thanos as a kind of almost hero, and don't actually know how to write a script for the Avengers in their conversations with Thanos.

All they're able to say is, *that's madness!*

But why is it madness, he says.

You don't know it's going to go that way. You can't make that decision. It's not yours to make.

Now, those are all true, it is madness—But *why?*

WITHOUT ARTICULATING FIRST PRINCIPLES AND FIRST VALUES, YOU CANNOT AROUSE OUTRAGE

Astonishment and outrage are aroused in response to the obvious violation of First Principles and First Values. If you can't actually articulate First Values and First Principles, you can't arouse astonishment and outrage.

- That's why when we saw George Floyd with Derek Chauvin's knee on his neck for nine minutes, in that complex and tragic story, we were beyond outraged, and we poured into the streets. Because we saw an obvious violation of value that pierced the slumber of the postmodern moment and aroused appropriate outrage.
- That's why in the first weeks of the Ukrainian war, when the media flooded our eyes with images of moral outrage, we were blown out of our minds, and we stood and we talked and we engaged.

Now notice, friends, I want you to notice this, take a look at the movie *Wag the Dog*.

Notice how, for a set of reasons, the media, in many ways, have looked away from Ukraine. How many of you thought about Ukraine in an active way in the last two weeks? Maybe a little bit, not much.

But Ukraine is in the middle of the worst throes of war right now. I'm tracking it very closely. How many people thought about Ukraine as much in the last two weeks as they did in the first six weeks of the war? Not so many, right?

Why? Because a set of decisions in the media establishment has moved your attention. You don't even realize it happened. But bracket that. That's a very, very important issue.

So, what we talked about last week was—and where we placed our attention is a place where people don't place their attention—we placed our attention on the shadows of transhumanism and the shadows of evolutionary spirituality, but not to dismiss these movements. (Those two, by the way, are not collapsible; they overlapped with each other. I don't want to collapse evolutionary spirituality and transhumanism, although they have lots of intersecting vectors). We talked about their shadows, not in order to dismiss them, but in order to point out that actually, there was some correctness in that critique of Barbara, which needs to be acknowledged.

But that acknowledgement has to fully understand that **Barbara was operating in that postmodern context in which there was an inability to articulate First Values and First Principles**, in which a Thanos kind of emergence was actually present in many, many conversations around the world. By the way, those conversations are still taking place around the world. There's still a strong transhumanist movement that's still having those Thanos conversations. That's why Thanos appeared as an ambivalent and complex figure in the 2018 and 2019 *Avengers* movie.

But we also wanted to point out last week that **Barbara herself *evolved* her position**. That was really the essence of our meeting at the Center for Integral Wisdom, we had an enormously deep set of tens and tens and tens of hundreds of conversations. Of course, the people who wrote that post critiquing Barbara ignored 130 or 140 weeks of One Mountain, in which Barbara's position, as Barbara and I integrated together, had clearly evolved. All of that was completely ignored.

In One Mountain, there are at least 130 to 140 episodes in the public space that show a very, very clear, unmistakable transformation and evolution of Barbara's own position. All of that material was completely ignored, because that's what happens when you cherry-pick sources to demonize someone in order to argue for a conspiratorial narrative, which actually has its own egoic agenda, which actually has its own set of vectors.

So, I really want to just honor Barbara in that way. It's what I wanted to do last week, and I want to deepen it this week.

Wow, that's a big introduction.

You understand we're doing this just for this week and next week, but this is wildly important.

MODELING EVOLUTIONARY CONVERSATIONS

I also want, if I can, to just honor Andrew Cohen. He's a peer and does not require my commendation, so I mean this not in a condescending way, but in a brother way – I want to really just honor him.

Andrew and I have exchanged a lot on this via WhatsApp, we had a very big exchange on this back in 2005 and 2006. Andrew wrote a book called *Evolutionary Enlightenment,* I wrote a book called *Self: Two Models of Self In Evolutionary Mysticism and Why They Matter.*

That book was a critique of Andrew's *Evolutionary Enlightenment* and what I thought were very clear flaws or shadows in the position of evolutionary spirituality. Since then, Andrew and I have had many deep conversations and, I believe, he dramatically evolved his position. He can speak for himself, he's perfectly beautiful and capable of doing that, but I welcome anyone to read that conversation. You can get the book *Evolutionary Enlightenment,* which is Andrew's book, which I think is, by the way, a great book. You can get my book, *Your Unique Self*, but particularly this book, *Self: Two Models of Evolutionary Mysticism*, which compares my Unique Self model with Andrew's authentic self model, and critiques the book *Evolutionary Enlightenment* in one particular regard.

I think, not only has Andrew's position dramatically evolved in this respect, and I think he took the critique seriously. But of course, in other areas, Andrew has impacted me. Because we engage as brothers in a kind of Dharma combat, but it's a combat in which we're loving each other, in which **we're honoring each other as peers, and we want to impact each other. That's what an evolutionary conversation is.** An evolutionary conversation is not *egos* jousting in the public sphere, in order to score points for their separate-self craving base, mad ego.

> *An evolutionary conversation is, we want to impact each other; we want to transform together.*

Just as Andrew allowed himself to be impacted and moved in a very deep way by *Self* and by many of our conversations, he shared that with me in phone conversations. There were dimensions of evolutionary spirituality and phrases that Andrew used such as, this particular phrase *ecstatic urgency*, which I love, and I've adopted, and I adduce it and cite Andrew. There were particular formulations of evolutionary spirituality that went through Andrew's prism and his unique experience that impacted me, and I'm delighted to say that. That's what we are supposed to do.

So, what Andrew and I just began doing is **we started a new public conversation on evolutionary spirituality.** We've done two conversations, and we've both spent a good deal of our lives trying to lay down different core tenets of evolutionary spirituality, and now we're coming together in a public conversation to share what we've done these last 20 years in this particular domain, and to evolve it further to be able to articulate it clearly.

That's how we need to have conversations.

- Can you imagine if the pro-life and pro-choice people got together and had those kinds of conversations?
- Can you imagine if the best of the Republican Party, George Will, and all of really the great figures in the Republican Party throughout the ages, got together with the best of the Democratic Party, in order to synergize?

As Jack Kennedy and Richard Nixon did in the late 50s, even into the early 60s. Even after their presidential debate, they remained close friends, as they should be, because they knew that they were each holding a piece of the puzzle, and that the puzzle only becomes whole when they love each other, when they become whole mates.

That's the way it's supposed to happen, and—we're so afraid to have a conversation!

An evolutionary conversation is when we're loving each other madly, and we're holding together this passion for truth, this passion for a deeper understanding, this passion for insight.

The people who just blow my heart open are people who can come and say:

> Hey, Marc. You said it this way. We've read the *dharma*, and we're in. But here's one dimension where I think there's one source that you could have taken into account, or where you could have looked at it this way, and you missed.

But not if they just *claim* it, but they actually go deep and they're fully engaged, and they bring to my attention, or they place my attention on something that I missed. Or even they correct something that I've held for 25 years, but they show me a deeper way of understanding that, not because they *claim it* but because they *do the work*.

That blows my heart open! I fall madly in love with that person! That's how we have to have conversations. We have to hold the paradox of our unique expression and not allow it to degenerate into polarization. Because:

Paradise is a paradox.

That's what paradise is, it's a paradox.

- It's the ability to hold the fullness of contradiction,
- and not have it become a degenerative polarization,
- but actually a fructifying synergistic emergence of a new wholeness, a new story, a new paradox.

Wow, that's what we're engaged in here. Last week and this week we're just putting in some energy and we're trying to model what these conversations need to be like.

It's a very different model than the posts you see that try to string together a bunch of material, and take it out of context, and not actually check, and investigate, and paint a full picture, and allow for evolution.

That comes from ego self. That's an ego self game.

At the same time, even when I read people engage in that ego self game, if they make a point that's legitimate, I want to open my heart and say: *Wow, that's right. That's a really good point. That critique was correct.*

But since Barbara wasn't here to speak for herself, and she asked me when she passed to hold this together with her, so just in deep love and respect and honor for Barbara, I took the liberty, because I've had hundreds of conversations with her about this, with her responding. Part of the response was: "Yes, you're right. I made a mistake there, and it was actually a tragic mistake. I didn't understand that, but now I do, and I've evolved my position."

Just madly delighted to be together with everyone, and just honored to be able to, together as a Unique Self Symphony, honor Barbara, and model what a different kind of conversation looks like.

Evolutionary Love Code:

> That which unites us is far greater than that which divides us. We are united in a shared Story of Value. That does not make us perfect expressions of that value. We are all imperfect vessels for the light; the imperfect vessels for the holy and broken *Hallelujahs*. We must move beyond demonization, to daemonization. It is only the loss of daemon that turns us into demon. When we are not inside the circle together, we place others outside the circle as a way of pretending that we're on the inside. Only a shared story based on First Principles and First Values serves as the ground for a global ethos for a global civilization.

What a gorgeous code!

There's so much to say about the code. But this week, with permission, I really just want to have the code as a general context, holding Barbara—beyond the inappropriate demonization—as daemon, as the beautiful sense of charism. **Charism means Divinity flowing through.** And that's true, beautiful Divinity flows and flowed through Barbara, that grounds this One Mountain.

SUBTLE MCCARTHYISM AND FEAR ON THE INTERNET

I want to share one more thing. Someone called me, who's a very, very wonderful human being, who's on our board, and said, "I think we need to really distance ourselves from Barbara, because there were these critiques."

My response to that, with lots of love, it's *[expletive deleted]*. I've made a promise to my dear friend here in One Mountain that there's no *[expletive deleted]* in *One Mountain*, so I won't tell you what I said.

But my point is, I can barely get the words out—**people are so afraid in the internet culture.** They're so afraid, and there's so much *subtle McCarthyism*. So, if someone's attacked, or if there's a move to cancel someone, what you've got to do is you've got to kind of back off of them, so you don't get tainted with that attack.

That is not the way we love in the world. **That is not who we are.**

I am so wildly proud that Barbara is my evolutionary partner, and our evolutionary partner, and that she grounded and founded *One Mountain, Many Paths* with us. The fact that Barbara made a set of early transhumanist mistakes in particular articulations, which I think were tragic, doesn't change that one iota at all.

I'm going to tell you something else. When in 2028, the dossier on Martin Luther King is revealed, (that's when it's going to be made public, at which time, if you've tracked this issue which I have, an enormous amount of very complicated, personal material about Martin Luther King is probably going to emerge), I am not going to demonize Martin Luther King. Because **Martin Luther King made a huge contribution, which was important and which was holy, and purity moved in his heart, and love moved him**—and he was a broken vessel for the light. Because we're all in some sense holy and broken *Hallelujahs*; we're all imperfect vessels for the light.

There's not a person alive who has greatness in them, who hasn't made mistakes that are real.

That's a very, very big deal. So, a person gets to make a mistake, and then gets to correct that mistake, and gets to transform.

There's an entire literature critiquing Martin Luther King on very, very powerful issues that are at the center of *MeToo*, and are at the center of honoring the feminine, but that doesn't mean that we dismiss Martin Luther King as a critical leader and we cancel him.

That's not what we do.

That's a very, very, very big deal! It's very easy also to misunderstand how we gather information. We don't gather information in internet posts which don't allow for genuine conversation and genuine truth searching.

But you have to look at how you gather information:

- Are you gathering information with an open heart?
- Are you open to receiving new information?
- Are you open to being impacted?
- Are you open to revising your position?
- Are you open to checking sources?
- Are you open to actually watching what your cognitive biases are, which move you to want to agree with a particular position?
- Are you open to checking where you're virtue-signaling or vice-signaling, in order to gain the approval of the crowd?

You've got to do all of that in order to engage in a source code conversation, in order to do evolutionary sensemaking.

We need to begin to understand that **how we gather information, and how we make judgments, was one of the great momentous leaps and breakthroughs of Evolutionary Love in modernity.**

But what's happening in postmodernity—I want to give you a big sentence if I can, with permission:

The exteriorization of the postmodern mind is the internet.

Meaning, the postmodern mind says, *there's no narrative, there's no story, there's no larger plotline.* For example, one of the things that the editor Kevin Kelley, who was representing the postmodern movement, argued is that we should no longer have books with authors. But all the information should be available, you just search it on the web, and should not be associated with an author and not associated with a particular book.

In other words, **that's the undermining of** *storyline*.

- So, we no longer hold in our memory long and complex threads of information, because we've actually outsourced memory itself to the internet.
- And when we read on the internet, we no longer stay in the deep thread of a plotline, because we're hyperlinking all the time.
- We no longer read as was described by Hawthorne in his *Sleepy Hollow*. He describes sitting against an oak tree and just going deep into reading. We don't do that anymore. But we actually search around on the internet.

My beloved Kristina described to me the difference between her experience that she had in her apartment in New York, a wall filled with books, and she describes her experience when she reads and when she's scrolling on her phone. She started doing a phone fast, in order to come back to straight reading, so you can actually drop *inside of the inside* as you read, and you allow a storyline to enter, and you allow information, and you begin to check the information.

But what we do today when we're scrolling, we are actually not engaged in *reading*. We're not engaged in a plotline. We're not actually able to organize information in our minds. We're jumping from source to source, we're hyperlinking. There's no narrative, there's no storyline, there's no plotline. And what we read is usually a particular vector or bubble of one of the sides in the propaganda wars, that are all saying something completely consistent, that never disagree with each other within that vector, which is how you know it's a vector of propaganda.

Wow, that's *not* how we do it! That's not how we form judgments.

So to those in my immediate circle who said, Barbara got a little critiqued, we need to back off, and maybe we shouldn't be publishing these books with Barbara—*are you kidding?!*

Are you kidding, my friends, my beloveds?!

We're going to embrace Barbara and honor her more than ever before.

Because we refuse to be hijacked by a techno-feudalist, neoliberal, postmodern hijacking of energy. The same way we're not going to be hijacked by a Trumpian corrupt narrative, we're not going to be hijacked by corrupt narratives on any side of the spectrum.

- We're going to look at every issue, and we're going to look at it deeply.
- We're going to do sensemaking together.
- We're going to gather contradictory opinions.
- We're going to check sources.
- We're going to check our heart and our body.

Then we're not going to *just talk softly*, we'll *talk fiercely*.

But we're going to integrate, we're going to synergize, we're going to get to new wholes. That's what we need to do all the time.

THE IRREDUCIBLE INFINITE VALUE OF UNIQUE PERSONHOOD

Now, I want to just hit one issue with you in terms of the mistake of early evolutionary spirituality and transhumanism, and I want to see if we can correct and evolve that mistake. I wrote several pages of notes to myself this morning, and we've gotten through the first three words, so I apologize for that. But as we move into fall, and we evolve the structure, we're going to be evolving the structure *One Mountain*, and we will have enough time to talk about everything. But let me just hit one issue.

The issue is, let's call it *the personal*.

So, when Thanos says, in order to save half of humanity, I'm going to destroy half of humanity, what Thanos doesn't understand is what we would call **the irreducible, infinite value of unique personhood.** That's huge!

So, for example, there's an entire literature which exists in the lineages of the great traditions, which asks the following question:

> If a city is being surrounded and attacked, and the attackers are willing to leave the city if the people inside the city will give up, let's say, five people to be the sacrificial victims, or even one person to be the sacrificial victim of those who are attacking? . . .

That's a major issue in the Hebrew lineage conversations, which revolves around a number of mythical stories that exist in the biblical canon: *Do you save a city by giving up one person?*

It's a more complex issue, but the general vector of conversation is: *absolutely not!*

That's complicated!

Absolutely not! We don't make that kind of calculation with a human life.

There's irreducible dignity to unique personhood.

Now, stay close with me. This is subtle. It's not simple. It's subtle, it's not simple. But of course, *why* is it not simple? Because we have something called war. Now, what's war?

So, I was sitting with the **Dalai Lama in Dharamsala,** who had invited me to visit him after an argument that I've told you guys about at different times, and we were talking about war. He said to me:

"People think I'm a pacifist, that I'm against wars, and it's not true. I think there should be an army; there needs to be an army. Because there are some issues that we can only handle, in a world that has despotic totalitarian dictatorships, we need to be able to at times respond with force."

Now, I agree with the Dalai Lama at this moment in history. To respond with force means: **we're willing to give up the lives of some young men, and in certain armies, young men and women, for the sake of keeping the larger whole safe.** So, it doesn't mean we never make a calculation.

I want to be very careful about this. It's actually a very subtle issue that requires an enormous amount of attention. We do at times make a calculation, and there are countries that have a draft, where someone can be *drafted* to go to war. They don't even get to make a choice about whether they participate in that war. Wow, that's not simple!

What does it mean for my son Eytan and my son Yair, who are both commanders in special forces in the Israeli army? What does it mean for them to literally risk their lives, to keep school buses safe in Israel, to keep them safe from blowing up? Why are they risking their lives?

Well, because **they're actually understanding themselves as part of the larger whole, and they're making a heroic decision that they are willing to risk their lives.** It's not that there's no conversation to be had, there *is* a conversation to be had, and it's got to be a subtle and careful conversation. But here's the point. You can't have the conversation absent First Principles and First Values.

CONVERSATION ABSENT FIRST PRINCIPLES AND FIRST VALUES IS IMPOSSIBLE

It's a subtle point, but it's everything.

In other words:

- **If you don't understand that every human life has infinite**

value, and that, in principle, it's worth giving up the entire city and not handing over one person
- If you don't understand that in your body
- **If you don't understand the irreducible dignity of every human story,** which is not just a separate-self story, but it's the Cosmos's story in person in that human being
- **If you don't know that that story has infinite value,** and it's precious beyond imagination, that every smile and every gesture of love by that person, and every expression of kindness and goodness, and every creative moment, and every jot and tiddle of pain and anguish, **that all of that matters infinitely and participates in the infinite Field of Person and Meaning**

If you don't get any oft his, **then you can't participate in a conversation about how you do trade-offs at the appropriate time.**

Because what you'll do is, as Stalin believed, as Mao believed, as Genghis Khan believed in his own way, what you'll basically do is you'll make a calculation which says:

I'm willing to give up, at the drop of a hat, hundreds of thousands of people, in order to accomplish my goal, whatever that goal is. Because I do a quick calculation, **I do a transhumanist calculation, and I operate in order to save humanity.** *I'm willing to give up a lot of it because it's a natural, logical calculation.*

No, actually...

Every human being is *all* of humanity, and *all* of humanity lives in every human being.

We have to start from the premise of the irreducible value of uniqueness.

We have to start from uniqueness as an ultimate value, from the irreducible value of an individual life, the irreducible value of the unique quality of intimacy that person incarnates

If I'm not living in the Field of Value, and I'm not living in the Field of First Values and First Principles, then there's no way to have the conversation. That's huge.

Now, clearly, we can't have the full conversation at this moment in time. But what we know is, the second you make a move towards eugenics, what you're doing is, you're 'solving' the problem the easy way.

The Thanos solution is actually the easy solution, and that's why the Avengers understand that Thanos is shortcutting. But they can't articulate why.

- He's shortcutting because he doesn't have First Principles and First Values.
- Because he doesn't have First Principles and First Values, he actually goes for the logical shortcut solution.
- The logical shortcut solution is, since there's not the irreducible dignity of every human life, what you do is in order to save half of humanity, you lose the rest of humanity, and you do it in a way that's painless.

But actually, there are many, many more creative possibilities on the table that Thanos has missed. **Our response to existential risk and our response to catastrophic risk is not to cull the herd.**

It's not that *evolution is not nice*, as early transhumanists said.

Evolution is the Love Story of the Universe.

That's the big realization that Barbara came to as we studied together, that evolution is the Love Story of the Universe. In the Love Story of the Universe, every individual love story matters. And when I focus my love and place my love's attention on a challenge, I get wildly creative. And that wild creativity is born of love. That creativity allows me to generate both new exterior and new interior technologies.

That is why, for example, there was the great prediction in the late 1960s that there would be a famine that would sweep the world, and the world would essentially collapse in exponentially unimaginable famines. But the exact opposite happened. The reason the exact opposite happened is because there was a young scientist in Mexico who developed a new way of fertilizing soil and working with soil and with crops, that allowed for exponential increases in the production of food. That's an *exterior* technological creative breakthrough.

But we need to do something even deeper:

- We need to make breakthroughs in *interior* technologies, and we need to change the very vector of the story itself.
- We need to *tell a new Story of Value*, of First Values and First Principles.
- That new Story of Value will *inform* where we place our resources.

TECH PLEX CREATIVITY NEEDS TO PARTICIPATE IN THE NEW STORY OF VALUE

Do you know how important data science is in the world to actually developing creative, impactful solutions for existential risk? **Do you know where most data scientists are spending their time? None of them, virtually none of them are spending their time actually engaging with existential and catastrophic risk.**

Do you know where virtually all the data scientists in the world are spending their time today?

They're working for Google. They're working for Facebook. They're working for TikTok. They're working for Microsoft. They're working for Apple.

These are all for-profit companies that are hoarding, not even investing back into the market, unimaginable profits. Most of them are not paying any kind of normal taxation, some are not paying taxation at all, because of legal loopholes.

Financial resources owned by Sergey Brin are $150 billion. Why does Sergey Brin need $150 billion, with all due respect, Sergey? Sergey is a good friend of a close friend of mine. So, *Sergey, love you, man. But yo, man, what are you thinking?* Google is engaged in a process of exponential power and profit, and they've actually siphoned off all of the data scientists, so much so that universities today can't find professors of data science, because no one wants the job, because making a couple of hundred thousand a year at a university doesn't compare with the golden handcuffs of the Google, Facebook, Twitter, TikTok, Microsoft, Oracle, or Apple package.

We've taken, for example, data science, which is a critical vector that we need to deploy in order to generate new possibilities of engaging catastrophic and existential risk.

We've siphoned off that critical creativity into a success 2.0 win-lose metrics, rivalrous conflict story like: *Let me actually make another $800,000 a year in order for me to succeed in my monadic separate-self dissociated existence, which is actually an optical delusion of consciousness.*

So, if that's where we're going, if that's the story we're telling, well, then the only solution is Thanos.

But if we tell a new story—what would it mean to tell a new Story of Value, where if you're an up-and-coming data scientist:

- You actually want to go work on the World Hunger Project.
- You want to work on a new form of micro-financing.
- You want to work on new forms of education.

- You want to work on using the tech plex to *generate* new forms of individuated Unique Self education and transformation that shock Reality and introduce a Unique Self utopia that's been unimaginable in history.

We're going to do that only if we create a new sense of vision, of virtue, a new sense of courage, a new sense of nobility, where we're called to be knights at the new Round Table.

We're called to go on a noble quest.

It would seem ridiculous to us to go and make $800,000 at Microsoft. What an utter waste of a lifetime, when I can take my tech plex creativity and apply it to the transformation of Reality, where we create a motivational architecture of nobility and honor and value, and we want to participate in that nobility and honor and value.

So, you begin to see it:

At the very center of that new motivational architecture, is the irreducible dignity of every human story.

Not just the therapeutic dignity, but what underlies the original impulse of therapy, which is that that *story matters*. That story is not just reorganizing the past, although that needs to be done.

It's the fullness of presence in the present, and it's that Unique Self responding creatively, and giving their unique gifts to the call of the future.

Oh my god, **that's what an evolutionary spirituality needs to look like**, where:

- I'm an Evolutionary Unique Self.
- I'm *Homo sapiens* who's evolved and has become a new human and a new humanity, *Homo amor*.

- I'm the Universe: A Love Story in person, creatively playing my instrument in Unique Self Symphony, as we're omni-considerate for the sake of the whole.

That's the vision.

That's wildly exciting, and what an insane delight to be here on *One Mountain, Many Paths* and to be working together in these source-code conversations! Barbara is with us in every second, and we're all together. We're all creating a Unique Self Symphony together. I'm madly delighted, as we move into prayer.

So let's just go into prayer and turn to the *Infinity of Personhood* in Cosmos, which we call God. God is not a cosmic vending machine.

God is our experience of personhood that we all participate in, exponentialized into infinity.

God is not just the Infinity of Power. God is the Infinity of Intimacy that both lives in us and holds us, and holds our irreducible dignity, and embraces our holy and our broken *Hallelujah*.

So we move into prayer.

Just let's open up. Let's pray together. Let's pray together for the new world that we so desperately need to usher in together.

So take us inside to the holy and broken *Hallelujah*, to prayer, to Leonard Cohen.

Music: Hallelujah by Leonard Cohen:

CHAPTER SIX

BARBARA MARX HUBBARD'S BIRTHDAY: THE EVOLUTION OF CONSCIOUS EVOLUTION

Episode 323 — December 18, 2022

ARE YOU READY TO AWAKEN AS CONSCIOUS EVOLUTION?

Our topic today is the evolution of Conscious Evolution. We will listen to Barbara on her birthday about Conscious Evolution, and then I'll share with you how Barbara and I evolved Conscious Evolution together in the last five years of her life.

EVOLUTIONARY LOVE CODE: YOUR CLARIFIED HEART'S DESIRE IS THE TUNING FORK OF YOUR UNIQUE SELF

> Your clarified heart's desire is the evolutionary impulse awake and alive in you, as you, and through you.
>
> Your clarified heart's desire is the tuning fork of your Unique Self.

THE NEXT STEP IN CONSCIOUS EVOLUTION

> Your Unique Self is the invitation and demand of the self-organizing universe that you choose joy, join genius, and play your instrument in the Unique Self Symphony.

Are you ready to be evolution? Are you ready to participate in the evolution of consciousness and culture? Are you ready to participate in the evolution of love? Are you ready to love deeper and wider than you ever have before? Are you ready to include something or someone in your circle of love who has always been on the outside? Are you ready to change, grow, and transform in the way that you have long given up on? Are you ready to be a dreamer? Are you ready to activate evolutionary love in you, as you and through you? Are you ready to be and become more than you ever thought possible? Are you ready to awaken as Conscious Evolution?

This is the heart of the revolution.

We are in Florence in the Renaissance, faced by the same moment that Florence was in, but much more intense. Florence—premodernity, the old medieval world is dying, the Black Death, the pandemic, and multiple threats are sweeping through a collapsing Europe and Asia. Modernity, with its dignities, hasn't yet been born.

And a group of people in Florence, *a very small group of people*, my friends, in Florence and some other parts of Italy, about a thousand in total, get together and they say:

We can see around the corner. We understand that as new forms of information, new technologies come online, it won't be enough to respond to the pandemics. It won't be enough to respond to the Dark Ages.

We won't be able to say *let there be light* through technology.

In order to even generate new information and new knowledge and new science:

- We need a new Story of Value.
- We need a new understanding of what the human being is.

- We need a new understanding of the human being's relationship to Source and to the Infinite.
- We need a new Universe story, a new story of identity, a new narrative of desire, a new story of power.

These new stories are not made-up stories; they're not conjectures. They are not like, *oh, let's just declare something*. But can we take together all of the leading-edge validated insights of all of the wisdom streams?

This is what da Vinci said, and Ficino. They said, **let's take everything we know—validated insights, not just declarations—*let's weave them together, and let's tell the new Story of Value, which will raise all boats and respond to the crisis.***

And to the precise extent that they succeeded, they birthed what we might call and what Habermas calls: *the dignities of modernity*, which were:

- Universal human rights
- The emergence of the feminine
- New ways of information-gathering, which birthed the scientific method
- The great abolition of slavery

All of these came from these new ways of understanding Reality, from these new First Principles and First Values embedded in a new Story of Value. So, to the precise extent that they got the storyline right, the story led in beautiful directions.

But they got some really key parts of the storyline wrong.

Not particularly da Vinci and Ficino, but the people who came after. David Hume, dimensions of Immanuel Kant, neo-Darwinism, logical positivism, contemporary existentialism.

And there's a thread, a direct line, through all those dimensions of thought, which were the very heart and center of modernity, which basically said:

value is not real, value is only a social construction, the human being is a glorified animal.

And of course the human being possesses animal, and should, but:

> *The human being is this momentous emergent leap.*

They misunderstood the animal world as well. They misunderstood the full beauty of the animal world and thought the animals were essentially almost the same as rocks.

They didn't understand in modernity that actually, **we need a genuine story of value, which is not materialist, in which meaning is real, in which everything emerges from consciousness, in which value is real.**

Without that, the center does not hold. Without that, you have emptiness, and in that emptiness, false stories emerge.

For example, the success story, that virtually every single person on this call, myself included, is enculturated in. *Am I successful? When I look in the mirror, am I successful? Am I beautiful in a particular superficial way, which is part of my success?* And Reality began to be governed by this success story, which is rivalrous conflict governed by win-lose metrics, because there was no better story being told.

That failure of Eros—that failure to articulate a story which is equal to the depth of our own self-knowing, which is equal to the depth of our own experience—**is the root cause for existential risk and catastrophic risk, which is risk to the very existence of humanity and to the nature of our humanity.**

Meaning, two kinds of risks.

- The actual death of humanity: extinction, which is quite a real genuine option.

- Or the death of our humanity: we actually upgrade algorithms and we downgrade human beings.

I want to really set our intention on this first night—tonight is Hanukkah Festival, the Festival of Lights, and we'll light candles together next week. And we're moving towards Christmas and New Year's. And I love Christmas, and I love New Years, and I love Ramadan, and I love Hanukkah—but in this moment, let's reset our intention, as we enter into the depths of winter, and love it open, and into this new 2023. Let's understand, **everything's at stake**.

You can, if you want to, turn back to your life and say,

- let me just do my spiritual transformation usual work,
- and do my usual meditation,
- and do my usual trauma work,
- and I'll go listen to Gabor Maté (which is a great idea; love you, Gabor) and it's all good, you can do that,
- and close into your particular world,
- and commodify your own psychological development as part of your own success story,
- and not understand yourself as part of the whole,
- and not feel the whole,
- and not feel the pulsing meta-crisis that's emergent in the very fabric of Reality.
- You can look away. You can bury your head in the sand, as 99% of humanity is doing now. Or you can decide:

No! I want to cross to the other side!

I want to participate in the emergence of the new human and the new humanity.

I want to transform from being *Homo sapiens* to *Homo amor*—and *Homo amor* is the new human and the new humanity who's omni-considerate for the sake of the whole.

So, what we're doing here is, we're in this depth of practice; we're doing the yoga, the practice here of becoming the new story. The yoga here is *telling* the new story and *becoming* the new story, *articulating* the First Values and First Principles and *becoming* the First Values and First Principles.

This is about you and me. Am I just a spectator here? Am I just observing?

Or am I a stakeholder, am I part of the story?

Barbara would always call me and say, let's make sure to invite people to become members this week, to contribute this week. Because people need to know that we can create this revolution only if we resource. And Barbara always said re-source: we enter into Source. And we give generously.

It's yours to the precise extent that you want to get involved and become a stakeholder and become a partner.

WE NEED INFRASTRUCTURE TO ARTICULATE THE NEW WORLD PHILOSOPHY AND RELIGION

You know, our parents and grandparents and great-grandparents—lots of them built churches and built synagogues. Most of us are not doing that.

We're doing podcasts. We're showing up online. But actually, *we're not taking the responsibility of building the infrastructure so we can vision the new world.*

And that's very often why the classical religions—even when they don't have good leadership—keep moving on, because there's the sense in at least part of the population, *we've got to make sure that the church has a roof, that it's got good heating, and that we pay our dues, because we need that.*

We desperately need One Mountain, Many Paths.

THE EVOLUTION OF CONSCIOUS EVOLUTION

We need this evolutionary synagogue, church, mosque, which is trying—

- to articulate a new world spirituality as a context for our diversity,
- to articulate a new world religion as a context for our diversity,
- to articulate a universal grammar of value as a context for our diversity.

I just want to invite everyone to step in! There's such joy in stepping in, because that's how it's going to happen. And take your part, take your seat at the table, begin to play your instrument in the Unique Self Symphony.

This is ours. This is our revolution!

BARBARA MARX HUBBARD ENGAGED LIFE WITH FULL PASSION EVERY DAY

I just want to say something about Barbara Marx Hubbard. I am madly in love with Barbara Marx Hubbard, and she is just an awesome being. She's no longer with us in this world. She's moved on to that next structure and phase of existence, which is a mystery to us. But we know, through much validated information, of the continuity of consciousness.

Barbara and I, together as evolutionary partners, founded this One Mountain, Many Paths. We originally called it Evolutionary Church. And you're going to hear from Barbara today. And Barbara said to me, dozens of times, *wow, this evolutionary undertaking, this One Mountain, Many Paths, this Evolutionary Church, this has to be the heart of the revolution. This is the place where we can actually tell the new story.*

And Barbara and I *wrestled* together. She came to find me in 2013 or 2014—someone introduced us—and we did a deep set of dialogues together which are online. She joined us at our Success 3.0 event, and then she read the Unique Self material, and lots of other things. She was at that time 84.

She said, *I don't know how much time I have left. But I understand that you and the people around you are holding the next evolution of Conscious Evolution, and you're holding some pieces I was missing. I want to bring to you the pieces I have, and let's join genius and co-create.* **Let's not join genes, let's join genius and co-create,** as Barbara loved to say.

She stepped in with full power, with full energy; and tornados were caused in many ways by the coming together of these energies; and an enormous goodness was created, and enormous creativity was unleashed.

And Barbara and I spoke—tears in my eyes—we communicated four or five times a day, literally, for those last several years. And Barbara was, quite literally, until the last several days when she was unconscious, Barbara was in full powerful cognizant form.

She went through very hard times in the last five years. She was often profoundly pained and lonely. Many of her best friends had passed away, and she felt, in a deep sense, alienated from different dimensions of her world. And in other ways, she was more alive and more on fire than ever.

Barbara would—literally every day—face the emptiness, and she'd work through it, and she'd walk through it. She'd call me and we'd talk, or we would exchange a text or a voice message. **Every single day, she literally recreated herself and lived the knowing that: we don't get older, we get newer.** And she had more energy pouring through her, and more delight, and more audacity, and more impishness, and more creativity, and more sense of "Let's renew it every day."

She would call me every day, or I would call her, and she would share with me a set of ideas that we had talked about, and that we both understood. But she would share them not because she forgot, it wasn't amnesia, but **she would share those ideas completely anew, as if we had never talked about them before, with full power and excitement,** *like a virgin for the very first time.*

THE EVOLUTION OF CONSCIOUS EVOLUTION

> *That's how we approach ideas, that's how we approach First Principles and First Values: we re-engage with full passion every day.*

And Barbara, I miss you enormously. I miss your radical positivity, and your willingness to move through the emptiness and to move through the pain, and your willingness to grow.

INTEGRATING BARBARA'S LEGACY INTO THE NEW STORY OF VALUE

Literally, we did Holy of Holies, private study together every single week. And she would always say, *Okay, how can I grow, how can I be more?* She would never say, *I know the First Principles, I know the Dharma.* No. *How can I learn this again? How can I read more? How can I embody more?*

Barbara was—and *is* in her next incarnation, but right now *was*—a great, great, great being, and I love her dearly, and loved her dearly, and I have mad depth and admiration and honor for all of her work.

Part of her capacity to grow was to understand, *we've got to go to the next stage.*

Barbara and I disagreed radically with how she was presenting Conscious Evolution for the first 30 or 40 years of her life. **Barbara didn't originate the idea of Conscious Evolution, but she became its primary champion.**

As we began to talk—and I challenged certain ways in which Barbara understood Conscious Evolution—she began to assimilate and integrate those. In the video you're about to see, Barbara and I had already been talking for two years. So, some of the core ideas we had talked about are integrated there, others aren't, but I want you to *really hear* Barbara, and then I'll share with you what Barbara and I together—joining genius—synergized, and how we brought this together in the last five years of her life.

And perhaps I can say one other thing, and I apologize, slightly insincerely, for being direct. There are a few people in the world who want to reframe Barbara as what she did her whole life *until* the last five years. But actually, that's not what Barbara wanted. Barbara viewed the last five years of her life as being wildly creative, wildly alive, wildly transformative and deepening. Because that was her integrity and her audacity. And I've made a commitment to Barbara to share these ideas with the world.

As we turn to Barbara, I want to say one more thing, which is, **we're actually looking to integrate Barbara's legacy into this new Story of Value. She left with the Center an entire sheath of unpublished documents that need to be integrated into the story.** They need to be curated and unpacked and downloaded. And of course, we don't have the resources to do all of that ourselves, so we're looking for someone to do that.

Some of us have done a brilliant job of recreating Barbara's website, *Foundation for Conscious Evolution.*[9] So we're going to give that site an entirely new emergence. And we're going to be talking there about the 1.0 version of Conscious Evolution in seven major ideas, and the 2.0 version of those ideas, which Barbara and I worked with together in the last five years.

So, without further ado, huge drumroll. The great, great spokesperson, I think the greatest spokesperson and the greatest storyteller of Conscious Evolution, in the second half of the twentieth century. I bring you my beloved evolutionary partner, Barbara Marx Hubbard.

CONSCIOUS EVOLUTION 1.0

Interviewer: What is conscious evolution?

Barbara: Conscious Evolution is evolution by choice, not chance.

---

9 Visit https://foundationforconsciousevolution.org.

THE EVOLUTION OF CONSCIOUS EVOLUTION

For billions of years, evolution has been progressing. We've had five mass extinctions, we've had billions of species extinct before we got here, but the interesting thing is that we are the very first species on planet Earth *aware of* our own evolution, we've *heard about* the billions of years of evolution.

We are the first species to know we are affecting our own evolution by everything we do: the babies we have, the food we eat, the cars we drive, the wars we fight, even the thoughts we hold about each other. We can see that we are affecting our evolution in such a manner that we might devolve; we might destroy our life support system, we might actually render ourselves extinct.

That amounts to the greatest wake-up call that humanity has ever had. Because no species has been responsible for its own evolution or evolution at large, we have no experience in this. But nonetheless, we're entering the first age of Conscious Evolution.

I believe in retrospect, when we look back on this age, it will be as great a breakthrough as self-reflective consciousness in the Neanderthal world was.

Interviewer: What is the social potential movement?

Barbara: We know what the *human potential* movement was. It was when Abraham Maslow, the psychologist, began to study human wellness rather than illness, and he identified a new kind of person. It was in the 1960s, and he called it a *self-actualizing human* who is somebody with self-rewarding work, that they find intrinsically valuable and of service.

When Maslow mapped the characteristics of the self-actualizing person, **we began to try to be self-actualizing.** And it started the *human potential* movement, the *transpersonal* movement. The whole *consciousness* movement was really started by that thought.

The *social potential* movement is the next step.

As he identified peaks of human wellness and got to the self-actualizing person, it was time to identify the peaks of social excellence, social innovation, social wellness.

If we could trace the peaks in health, education, economics, science, technology, energy, and government that are working at the highest level, **we would have the beginning of the self-actualizing society.**

My book, *Conscious Evolution: Awakening Our Social Potential*, is an early contribution to the self-actualizing society. And if that self-actualizing person takes hold, we will begin to see more of us working to actualize our social potential.

Interviewer: What do you mean, problems are evolutionary drivers?

Barbara: It's very obvious. We find it in our own personal lives, and we find it in the life of the larger social system.

Problems are evolutionary drivers.

Because you either solve them by doing better and changing something, or they do you in. Another phrase is: **Crises precede transformation.** In evolution, when you look at the billions of years of transformation, almost every time there is a quantum jump of a higher order—from single-celled, to multi-celled, to animal, to human—you will find a series of crises to the life form just before the jump.

The way nature takes jumps through crises and problems is this mysterious function of being able to connect separate parts to make a new whole, greater than the sum of its parts.

And you can see right now, our culture is under stress.

- ♦ We have a crisis to our entire environment.
- ♦ We have a crisis with global warming.
- ♦ We have the possibility of running out of fresh water.
- ♦ We are endangered.

THE EVOLUTION OF CONSCIOUS EVOLUTION

What is that doing? It's making us realize that we have to change our economic system, our political system, and our war machine. It means we're going to have to learn to cooperate. So, if you jump over the crisis and imagine us being able to respond co-creatively, I think we're going to see a much better future and a much better humanity. **The threat of our devolution and extinction—that's the driver.**

Interviewer: You speak of evolution as guided by spirit in action, with a tendency towards higher consciousness, freedom, and order.

Barbara: There is a very deep controversy in the way people look at the meaning of evolution.

- The materialistic, scientific, modernistic view of evolution is that it is a random process, guided by accident and physical laws. And as you get up to life, it is through error and random mutation, and the process of natural selection, and reproductive advances, that lead to this entire universe.
- The other view is that consciousness is primary, and out of consciousness has come the emergence of energy, matter, life, and consciousness force.

The genius of evolution is consciousness in action, that has led not as a god outside manipulating things, but as a process of trial and error, and meandering and mistakes, and many, many extinctions.

But nonetheless, you can't look at the spiral of evolution without seeing that it's going somewhere. When we hit a crisis, we seem to move to higher order, to more complexity, to more freedom, to more consciousness, to more synergy, to more complexity and more love.

The exciting part for us is that **we are expressions of that intelligent universe, hopefully being awakened from within by that creative intelligence, to become more intelligent, more conscious, more creative, more loving, more synergistic**, which would mean that instead of everything being in a separate silo, like healthcare, or religion, or science and technology, we'd have *synergy*—the coming together of separate parts in our society—*to make a greater whole system that's far greater than the sum of our parts.*

So, it's very important how we interpret evolution.

As a co-creator, you feel the evolutionary impulse in you to be more creative. When you feel that, you don't feel it's just your personal whim.

- You feel you're participating with a greater force for a greater purpose.
- And you feel that your inner drive to express yourself is part of the noble purpose of the Universe itself.

Interviewer: What can an individual do about all this? How do I participate personally in conscious evolution?

Barbara: How do I participate personally in conscious evolution? That is a very good question.

Some people say to me, *Barbara, you think you are going to influence evolution?*—looking at me like I was crazy. And I say, *Yes, everybody is influencing evolution.*

And if you think of us at a tipping point—when we could go to devolution and destruction, or evolution and higher levels of creativity—what you realize is that **every single person is influencing the tipping point.**

- If you're very depressed and you're going down, you're helping the tip that way.
- If you're activated and realizing your own motivation, your own life purpose, your own inner drive, if you're saying *Yes* to creative action, vocation of destiny, life purpose…

…that is what the individual can do:

> Identify what attracts you, what you most deeply want to express, to become, and to give, and say the big *Yes* to that.

Then you have to reach out, you have to find others who are attracted to you, whom you are attracted to, and you have to begin to co-create.

And at the highest level of co-creation, you discover vocational arousal; you are excited if somebody needs what you most deeply want to do or give, so that you can join genius with others. As we join genes to have the baby, now we're having fewer children and living longer and longer lives, we can join our genius.

And when you do, with two or more, you find you're more than you ever were before, and you've given more to the Universe.

I mentioned Abraham Maslow's study of self-actualizing people, all of whom had one trait in common: self-rewarding action, or vocation they found intrinsically self-rewarding and of service.

So in order to participate in evolution, it's defined not just as a job or a project, but as an expression of your own creativity, such that **when you offer it into the world, it's of service to others, and you feel rewarded in the creativity of it.**

We used to think that creativity was only with artists or writers or very, very special geniuses. But actually, everybody has a Unique Self; everybody has a unique gift to give; whether it's a mother, a farmer, a gardener, a futurist, a scientist—the key is, it's self-rewarding, it's of service, you are rewarded in the doing of it, and that is your greatest contribution to Conscious Evolution.

CONSCIOUS EVOLUTION 2.0: I AM CONSCIOUS EVOLUTION IN PERSON

Thank you, Barbara, that was just completely beautiful.

And now, let's go the next step. I mean, whenever I see Barbara, and I see her often—I miss you deeply, Barbara. Now, let me share with people what we did.

THE NEXT STEP IN CONSCIOUS EVOLUTION

This conversation that you just heard from Barbara was recorded around 2015. You notice she was already talking about Unique Self and unique gift, because she had just actually read the Unique Self book. We started talking in 2013, so this was a couple years later. But before we'd gotten into the depths. Now stay close, friends. I'm going to try and take this wild ride.

So, Barbara, at this point in the conversation was mid-emergence of this next stage of Conscious Evolution, which is the core of what we're doing here at the Center: The new Story of Value of CosmoErotic Humanism.

So, Barbara starts the conversation by saying: *Conscious Evolution is evolution by choice, not chance.*

That is *precisely incorrect!*

And that's what Barbara I worked with, and Barbara and I actually transcended that sentence. And that was the standard sentence that she had used for 30 years.

In that, she was similar to people like, let's say, Brian Swimme, who worked with Thomas Berry— and did and is still doing enormously good work in the universe story. Brian and I have communicated; we've never quite been able to sit and talk, but we're aware of each other's work. And Brian has done fantastic work with Mary Evelyn Tucker. But particularly, in Brian's work as a mathematical cosmologist, what Brian does is he adopts, time and again, the standard neo-Darwinian narrative of evolution by chance, random mutation, natural selection. That neo-Darwinian synthesis is dead in science. It's an old neo-Darwinian synthesis, which at the major time that Brian was writing, you couldn't break with, but it needs to be broken with. Not to any form of intelligent design, a superimposed intelligent design, but to a much deeper understanding of the Universe story.

So, Brian did the same thing that Barbara was doing here, where Barbara says: Conscious Evolution is evolution by choice, not by chance.

That's precisely where we evolved. That is to say, **evolution doesn't first become conscious through human beings.**

Evolution did not manifest mitosis and meiosis, evolution did not manifest the chlorophyll molecule (try and work out what the chlorophyll molecule is, it's shocking) through a random process which was pure accident, without any sense of intrinsic meaning. Rather, **a deeper understanding of science is that there *is* value and meaning, all the way down and all the way up the evolutionary chain.**

Now, does that mean that atoms experience meaning like human beings do? No, it doesn't!

My colleague, Zachary Stein, and I have articulated a very deep understanding of the radical continuity of value, all through matter, life, and mind, and the discontinuity of it. How at every level of matter, there's a new emergence of value. And you jump from matter to life, from the physio sphere to the biosphere, there's an even deeper emergence, a jump to a deeper understanding of value. And when we emerge from the biosphere—life—to the depth of the self-reflective human, then meaning and value evolve.

So, there's both continuity of value and meaning all the way from matter to life to mind, and there's discontinuity. But there is value and consciousness and meaning, all the way up and all the way down the evolutionary chain. That's clear.

Meaning, evolution before the human being wasn't evolution by chance.

There is an inherent consciousness to evolution, there's a LoveIntelligence, without which it is impossible to make sense of Cosmos.

We're not talking about a cosmic vending-machine caricatured creator god, who wants to make sure that you're having proper sex which is appropriately heterosexual and doesn't have any sense of that which is beyond classical gender. Not that, that's not what we're talking about.

We're talking about an inherent LoveIntelligence of Cosmos that clearly has direction. There's telos. There are *inherent* First Principles and First Values, which are the plotlines of the Universe story.

Does everyone get that? That's insanely exciting.

Barbara brought me together with my dear friend Howard Bloom, who understands himself as being alienated completely from the world of Spirit, kind of a hardcore scientist; in some sense, one of the hidden scientific gurus of the space program, widely published.

In our first conversation, Barbara asked me to share this new set of ideas with Howard that had so animated her, where we began to understand that Conscious Evolution doesn't mean that evolution becomes conscious. There is some dimension of the evolutionary process that's always been conscious.

Conscious Evolution means that we as human beings become awake, aware, and alive, and realize that evolution is moving through us, that we are irreducibly unique expressions of the evolutionary process.

I realize that the evolutionary impulse moves uniquely in me, and *my awareness of that, my awareness that I am evolution, is a new emergent.*

As I pointed out in beautiful conversations with Barbara for many hours, there are antecedents to that idea that live in the interior sciences. That idea is actually present. But that idea is validated through evolutionary science, where I realize that every muon and every hadron and every lepton and every proton, neutron and electron, every atom and every molecule, and every macro-molecule, and all of the stages of organismic evolution, they all live in me.

- All of the physiosphere, all of matter, all of the biosphere, all of life actually lives in me.

THE EVOLUTION OF CONSCIOUS EVOLUTION

- All previous structure stages of humanity live in me.
- And so, *I don't live in evolution; evolution lives in me.*
- That's a momentous leap, that awareness. So, the notion of Conscious Evolution 2.0 is:

I awaken as the realization that I am Conscious Evolution in person.

That's number one. Conscious Evolution means that *evolution is animated by Eros.*

Number two, I *realize* in Conscious Evolution that evolution is animated by Eros. And this is something you might have noticed in Barbara's talk, in the second part of the talk, she said: The most important question is— which was unresolved, pretty much until 2015—*how do we understand the evolutionary story?*

Is the evolutionary story, a story of evolution by chance? Which is how Barbara began the conversation and affirmed that—which is incorrect. But in the second part [of the video above], she was already considering the deeper conversations we were having, about evolution being a coherent process animated by intelligence.

And she understood very deeply that everything rests on resolving that question.

And we can't resolve that question by declaration, we can't resolve it by faith.

We have to resolve it by actually telling a new Story of Value, where we go so deep into the evolutionary sciences, where we actually read the science so deeply that science begins to tell the story of the Eros of evolution; that we actually understand that evolution is animated by Eros, it's animated by Evolutionary Love, and that...

I, as a human being, am Evolutionary Love in person. Evolution is the progressive deepening of intimacies, and that intimacy means something.

NEXT STEPS TOWARDS CONSCIOUS EVOLUTION 2.0

I'm going to hold here. All of this is what we spent the last five years on, and I can tell you, Barbara was ecstatically excited about it, contributed an enormous amount to it, and it reconfigured her own understanding of Conscious Evolution. So, the conclusion would be,

> Conscious Evolution is not that evolution becomes conscious.

Evolution was always conscious.

Conscious Evolution is:

- I become aware that evolution is conscious in me,
- I become aware that I am evolution.
- I become aware of the entire story of evolution.
- I can locate myself, and I can look at my story as chapter and verse in the evolutionary story.
- I understand that evolution is animated by Eros, and therefore my story is a love story.
- I understand that my love story is chapter and verse in the love story of evolution, that evolution is the love story of the universe.

I'm wildly excited to share that Barbara and I, together with Zak Stein, we'll be sharing a group of five volumes that tell that story that we've been working on for the last four years. That's wildly exciting! And Barbara, that's such deep honor to you, and such a deep love for you, and such deep delight. Thank you, everyone, for joining us.

CHAPTER SEVEN

THE EVOLUTION OF CONSCIOUS EVOLUTION: CELEBRATING BARBARA MARX HUBBARD, MY EVOLUTIONARY WHOLE MATE

Episode 392 — April 14, 2024

RE-VISIONING CONSCIOUS EVOLUTION

Today, we are having a big Barbara Marx Hubbard celebration, because it is Barbara's birthday. Barbara, I love you madly, my evolutionary partner and whole mate. We celebrate your birthday every year, and there is no way we are going to miss it. We're going to celebrate Barbara and hear from Barbara.

There is a very deep relationship between a person's birthday and the day that they passed. It's very deep. Barbara was born December 22nd, 1929. That's her birthday. She passed on April 10th, 2019. I was at the bedside when she drew her last breath.

April 10th, 2019. Five years ago? Is that five years ago, my friends? I can't quite believe that it's five years ago. Eighty-nine unimaginable years. The day of my birth and the day of my death—this portal into the world and

this portal out of the world, this sacred and wondrous time—are so deeply related. David, the master of the lineage, dies and is born on the same day. It's a special privilege.

Barbara made a decision. Her decision was—I would say it was her last huge creative decision—to say *yes* to this invitation issued by Reality itself: to start this Evolutionary Church, to start this *One Mountain, Many Paths*. I remember calling Barbara and talking to her about this. Her first response was, "A church? Religion?" And then we went deep into it together, and we realized this was the only thing that could be done. It's what *needed* to be done. We stepped into it. Barbara and I together, as evolutionary whole mates, launched this adventure—and we are now on week 392.

What's the purpose?

Why do we have an Evolutionary Church, which we named *One Mountain, Many Paths*?

We have it in order to realize that value is real. **I would say that the most exciting dimension of the last five years of Barbara's life was the realization that value is real.** It's a very big deal.

There were many people in Barbara's world, people in her family and people around her, who told her—she would tell me all the time—"Hang up your cleats." Meaning, you're done. You're 82, you're 83. You've done so much.

- You did such a great job, you've been the great storyteller of Conscious Evolution.
- You've started SYNCONs, which were these wonderful conferences designed to bring the vision of Conscious Evolution into the world.
- You've been the great evangelist of Conscious Evolution.
- You gave a speech at the Democratic National Convention in 1984, where you were a symbolic candidate for vice president.
- You conceived this vision of the Office for the Future. The Office for the Future is now holding the vision of everything,

the *One Mountain, Many Paths* and the think tank, the Center for World Philosophy and Religion, and the Foundation for Conscious Evolution. All of that is under the umbrella of the Office of the Future. Barbara conceived this vision of the Office of the Future.

So everyone told you, "Hang up your cleats." Why didn't Barbara hang up her cleats? Why didn't you just say, *I'm done*?

People around her were saying, *She's impulsive, she can't stop*. No, it wasn't that at all. It wasn't this inability to stop. It wasn't impulsiveness. It wasn't a desire to stay relevant in some way. It's that **Barbara wasn't getting older. Barbara was getting** *newer.*

That was Barbara's actual experience, and it wasn't just an existential experience. What happened is: Barbara stepped into—together with me, we did it together—she stepped into this deeper world which took her understanding of Reality to the next level. It completely changed the way she understood Conscious Evolution. We re-understood, we re-visioned Conscious Evolution *together*. It's a very big deal. We literally re-visioned Conscious Evolution.

EVOLUTION IS THE SYNERGY OF RADICAL *TELOS* AND COMPLETE FREEDOM

The way Barbara had always taught Conscious Evolution is: *evolution by choice, not by chance*. There are a thousand talks online of Barbara saying that. But we went deeper.

What does *Conscious Evolution* actually mean?

Evolution is *never* by chance—and evolution has full freedom.

Conscious Evolution is not: *Oh, evolution was a chance process, and now the human being is awakened. Now it's not a chance process, because we are in the age of the Anthropocene—the human is at the center—so, what we do determines the future.*

That's how Barbara taught Conscious Evolution. That was the way it was taught all over the world. It is a powerful realization. It is true, but it's extremely partial—because **it's not true that evolution used to be by chance.**

Evolution is something far more beautiful. And the move to Conscious Evolution is therefore a different move.

So, what *is* evolution? I am just going to give an example.

I was doing Holy of Holies with this new person; we've gotten to know each other in the last couple of years. Last Saturday, we did this very deep dive, very beautiful. It was graced by Goddess, every step of it. And we said at the end, *Wow, if we get a transcript of what we just talked about in the last hour, we will see that everything we talked about is in perfect synchronicity, in perfect symmetry, in perfect design.*

Many of us who do Holy of Holies can attest to the exact same experience— that it was perfectly designed. And yet, we didn't spend even one minute designing it. Had we *tried* to design it, it would have taken us like four years to design every moment in it.

Why? Because what designed it was the First Principles and First Values that we were operating within, which were the fundament, the basic structure, the universal grammar of value. We shared between us this grammar of value, this desire to participate in the Evolution of Love, this knowing that love and Eros are real. There was a whole set of understandings in the shared space between us, rooted in two things:

- The shared set of First Principles and First Values
- The realization that the values themselves are real

These are real values. These are not arbitrary. We are, in some sense, invited by, defined by, animated by—not *constrained* in a negative sense, but directed by, or *allured* by—the shared set of First Principles and First Values. We are looking together in the same direction.

In Holy of Holies, we are not just soul mates looking into each other's eyes. We are whole mates—we are looking in a shared direction.

And because we are looking at a shared horizon—animated, and allured, and invested, and suffused with these shared First Principles and First Values—what emerges is the most elegant design you could possibly imagine—and yet completely spontaneous, completely contingent, radically new, radically novel, radically emergent.

- It's not the old premodern religious position in which God is sitting and saying, "Okay, do this, and do that, and do that." It is all preordained and eternal, and there is no freedom, and there is no emergence. We are just playing out a prewritten script. That clearly is not the interior nature of evolution.
- At the same time, it's not a postmodern deconstructive world, which is purely materialist, and evolution is a process of pure reductive materialist mechanics that's utterly chance and random.

No, evolution is not by chance. It was never by chance. **Evolution is an expression of the precise synergy.** It's the synergy of radical intention, *telos*, **direction**—the direction is the plotlines of cosmos, and the plotlines of cosmos are First Principles and First Values that are real—**and complete freedom, complete openness, complete new possibility, complete emergence, complete novelty.**

Evolution is the creative advance of novelty animated by First Principles and First Values that are real.

Wow! Now we begin to understand what Conscious Evolution is.

PLOTLINES OF EVOLUTION AWAKENING IN US

Conscious Evolution is *not* the move from evolution by chance to evolution by choice. **Conscious Evolution means that the First Principles and First Values of Reality come alive in** *me* **and in** *we*—**and we are now aware that** *we are* **First Principles and First Values** *in person.*

It is the move from the inherent values of evolution operating at the foundational levels of the evolutionary process—like Eros being real, and evolution reaching for ever deeper intimacy, and freedom, and personhood, and uniqueness, and transformation, and creativity—to becoming *aware we are* First Principles and First Values in person.

Conscious Evolution means I realize I am the evolutionary impulse animated by plotlines called First Principles and First Values, in person. **I am an irreducible, unique incarnation of the plotlines of the cosmos.**

That's exciting. Because what that means is I'm not just *making up* value. Value is real. Barbara's crazy delight was this realization: Everything I'd done up to now in my life was perfect, and now we can take it to the next level, and realize that evolution is actually a mystery, and often we don't understand it. But it's a mystery within the context of an Intimate Universe in which intimacy itself is a value. It's reaching towards ever greater wholeness—and wholeness is value. It's reaching towards ever greater value—and value is real. Wow! That's Conscious Evolution!

Let's say it a little better. There are values of Cosmos at its foundational levels—in the world of matter. In the world of matter, you have Eros and allurement between subatomic particles that creates a new intimacy, a new wholeness, a new value called an atom.

But that same intimacy evolves. It gets deeper. It gets wider. It gets thicker. The intimacy between us—between beloveds today, or between participants in the Unique Self Symphony, and the intimate communion of the Unique Self Symphony with a shared vision that participates in:

- A wider and deeper degree of freedom
- A more conscious sense of uniqueness
- A more radical creativity
- A more profound sense of choice than the intimacy between subatomic particles

All of the values of cosmos are at play all the way up and all the way down the evolutionary chain (in subatomic particles, or early plants, or early fish, or early animals, and then early mammals), but they become more and more conscious, more and more awake.

They become more and more awake *in us*, to be more precise.

In other words, **the entire process of evolution is self-evidently intelligent and conscious.** A non-intelligent and non-conscious process does not generate mitosis and meiosis before there's a human neocortex. It doesn't generate photosynthesis before there's a human neocortex. The process of photosynthesis, which is shockingly, dazzlingly complex—we've barely begun to get a glimmer of even vaguely understanding it—takes place billions of years before there is a human frontal lobe or neocortex.

That doesn't happen from an unintelligent mechanical accident.

That has nothing to do with fundamentalist versions of intelligent design. Intelligent design is wrong in the sense that it often (although not always) denies that there is an inherent process of creativity that's constantly evolving. There are many versions of intelligent design that deny that, and that's a mistake. There is no intelligent design in a fundamentalist sense— **but there is an inherent consciousness and intelligence in Reality that contains what we might call design principles.** DNA is a code. A code has design principles. There are no design principles and a code—ever—that don't come from some kind of inherent intelligence and consciousness.

Conscious Evolution evolved. That was our wild excitement.

THE WAY WE MEET BARBARA IS BY SHOWING UP IN OUR FULL SELVES

It was sad to Barbara—she talked to me about it literally every day—that *her family didn't get it*. They just didn't get it: *What are you doing? Hang it up. Hang it up, mom.* Her friends over the years: *What are you doing? You've done it already. You've achieved victory.*

This is what she would tell me. She would call me every day, and she would say, this person or that person or that person would say to her, "Barbara, declare victory and go home."

But *Barbara was not getting older. She was getting newer*—her phrase. She was madly excited to be alive as an evolutionary whole mate. She knew what evolutionary family meant. And she was madly committed to every single person who is here today, and to the existence of *One Mountain, Many Paths*, and to its unfolding in the world.

You are in her space. You are in her bosom now. You are in her embrace. Is that fair, Barbara? Is that fair, love? That's fair.

We're madly celebrating Barbara Marx Hubbard; we're madly celebrating evolution alive in person as Barbara Marx Hubbard—the stunning vision of evolution.

There could be nothing that would make Barbara more ecstatic than this book, *The First Values and First Principles*. And if I would turn to Barbara now, and I would say to Barbara now, or she'd be texting me now and she would say, "Marc, we've really got to talk to everyone, so they get to participate."

The way we meet Barbara is by showing up in our full selves and transcending the limits of our contraction, the limits of our collapse. Because everyone has reasons to contract. Barbara transcended every day the limits of her collapse. It's not that we can always do it, but we can do it a lot more than we think.

THE EVOLUTION OF CONSCIOUS EVOLUTION

We actually step in, and:

- All of a sudden, we're filled with power
- All of a sudden, we're filled with joy
- All of a sudden, we're filled with this realization: I am Conscious Evolution in person

We are celebrating—wildly celebrating—Barbara Marx Hubbard. We're going to see a little clip now. This is a tradition we do every year on the anniversary of Barbara's passing.

It's both her birthday and the day of her death. It's her birthday into the next world.

In the lineages, birthday and the day of death are the same. We call them the same thing. They are called by a name that indicates both being born and passing. You're being born into the next world, and you're passing. And they are happening together.

We're just going to spend like just three minutes, and we're going to feel into the space. We'll feel into Barbara Marx Hubbard.

[Morning Has Broken: Clip Playing for Barbara]

Oh my God! Oh my God! Barbara, we miss you, love. We miss you. I miss Barbara every day. I miss Barbara. Thank you for being our beloved. And thank you for being my whole mate. And thank you for being all of our whole mates. Thank you for being with us. Thank you for everything.

Barbara, this is your home. This is your home.

APPENDIX: SONGS

THE BATTLE HYMN OF THE REPUBLIC—JULIA WARD HOWE[1]

Mine eyes have seen the glory of the coming
of the Lord.

He has trampled down the vintage
where the grapes of wrath are stored.

He has loosed the fateful lightning
of his terrible swift sword.

His truth is marching on.

HOW COULD ANYONE—LIBBY RODERICK[2]

How could anyone ever tell you
you were anything less than beautiful?

How could anyone ever tell you
you were less than whole?

How could anyone fail to notice
that your loving is a miracle—
how deeply you're connected to my soul?

---

1 Julia Ward Howe, "The Battle Hymn of the Republic," 1862.
2 Libby Roderick, "How Could Anyone," on *If You See a Dream* (Turtle Island Records, 1990), CD.

APPENDIX: SONGS

I WANT TO KNOW WHAT LOVE IS—FOREIGNER[3]

I've gotta take a little time,
a little time to think things over.
I better read between the lines,
in case I need it when I'm older.
(Whoa, ooh-ooh, ooh-ooh)

And this mountain, I must climb
feels like the world upon my shoulders,
and through the clouds, I see love shine,
it keeps me warm as life grows colder.

[Pre-Chorus]
In my life, there's been heartache and pain.
I don't know if I can face it again.
Can't stop now, I've travelled so far
to change this lonely life.

[Chorus]
I wanna know what love is.
I want you to show me.
I wanna feel what love is.
I know you can show me.
Oh, oh-oh, oh (ooh)

I'm gonna take a little time,
a little time to look around me.
I've got nowhere left to hide,
it looks like love has finally found me.

[Pre-Chorus]

[Chorus]

[Outro]

(And I wanna feel) I wanna feel what love is

---

3 Foreigner, "I Want to Know What Love Is," recorded November 1984, on *Agent Provocateur*, Atlantic Records, vinyl LP.

(And I know) I know you can show me.
Let's talk about love.
(I wanna know what love is) The love that you feel inside.
(I want you to show me) And I'm feelin' so much love.
(I wanna feel what love is) No, you just cannot hide.
(I know you can show me) Yeah.
I wanna know what love is (Let's talk about love).
I want you to show me, I wanna feel.
(I wanna feel what love is) And I know, and I know.
I know you can show me (Yeah).
(I wanna know what love is) (I wanna know)
(I want you to show me) I wanna know, I wanna know, wanna know.
(I wanna feel what love is) (I wanna feel)
(I know you can show me).

HALLELUJAH—LEONARD COHEN[4]

Now, I've heard there was a secret chord
that David played, and it pleased the Lord.
But you don't really care for music, do you?
It goes like this, the fourth, the fifth,
the minor fall, the major lift.
The baffled king composing Hallelujah.

[Chorus]

Hallelujah, Hallelujah,
Hallelujah, Hallelujah.

Your faith was strong, but you needed proof.
You saw her bathing on the roof.
Her beauty and the moonlight overthrew you.
She tied you to a kitchen chair,
she broke your throne, and she cut your hair,
and from your lips she drew the Hallelujah.

---

4 Leonard Cohen, "Hallelujah", *Various Positions*, Columbia Records, 1984, LP.

[Chorus]

You say I took the name in vain,
I don't even know the name,
but if I did, well, really, what's it to you?
There's a blaze of light in every word,
it doesn't matter which you heard,
the holy or the broken Hallelujah.

[Chorus]

I did my best, it wasn't much.
I couldn't feel, so I tried to touch.
I've told the truth, I didn't come to fool you.
And even though it all went wrong,
I'll stand before the Lord of Song
With nothing on my tongue but Hallelujah.

OM NAMAH SHIVAAYA

Om Namah Shivaaya
Shivaaya namaha,
Shivaaya namah om
Shivaaya namaha, namaha Shivaaya
Shambhu Shankara namah Shivaaya,
Girijaa Shankara namah Shivaaya
Arunaachala Shiva namah Shivaaya

I bow to the soul of all. I bow to my Self. I don't know who I am, so I bow to you, Shiva, my own true Self. I bow to my teachers who loved me with love. Who took care of me when I couldn't take care of myself. I owe everything to them. How can I repay them? They have everything in the world. Only my love is mine to give, but in giving I find that it is their love flowing through me back to the world...I have nothing. I have everything. I want nothing. Only let it flow to you, my love... sing!

INDEX

A

alive, xiv, xxi, 1, 8, 29, 31, 38, 39, 41, 44, 46, 49, 53, 54, 58, 98, 104, 127, 139, 146, 148, 156, 164, 166
All-That-Is, xxix, 26, 33, 47
allurement, xvii, xxxvi, xxxviii, 3, 8, 15, 16, 164
Amorous Cosmos, 3, 78, 190
ani, 32
anthro-ontological, xxx, 40, 41, 43, 48
anthro-ontology, 38, 45
apocalypse, 112, 116, 117
Ark of the Covenant, 79
arousal, xxiii, 13, 153
asi, 57
atman, 37
atom, xxxviii, 156, 164
atomic, 17
atomic bomb, 17
atoms, 155
autonomy, 73
awaken, xxix, 14, 139, 140, 157
awakened, 59, 72, 80, 104, 151, 161
aware, 42, 68, 72, 102, 109, 118, 149, 154, 156, 158, 164

B

beauty, xxvi, 9, 29, 30, 40, 56, 65, 83, 97, 105, 109, 112, 115, 142, 170

Big Bang, 15, 30, 100
biosphere, 155, 156
blood, 35, 36, 65
body politic, 95
Brahman, 37
brain, 30
breath, 51, 100, 101, 159
Buddhism, xviii, 90, 91, 93
bypass, 87, 91

C

calling, xxiii, 2, 34, 86, 101, 112, 160, 190
capacities, 191
catastrophic risk, 25, 54, 82, 112, 134, 135, 142
Catholic, 35, 62, 66, 68, 69, 70, 105
Center for World Philosophy and Religion, iv
certain, 9, 68, 70, 72, 83, 88, 89, 90, 91, 92, 96, 113, 114, 115, 118, 132, 147
certainty, 49, 50
chakra, 100, 104
chant, 21, 30, 31, 32
children, 50, 60, 153
choice, xxii, xxviii, xl, 48, 102, 124, 132, 148, 154, 161, 164, 165
Christ, 26, 34, 35, 37, 39, 41, 44, 45, 47, 58
Christianity, 105

INDEX

Christmas, 1, 4, 143
circle, xxvii, 5, 6, 7, 8, 13, 14, 15, 41, 50, 64, 68, 92, 94, 98, 126, 130, 140
clarity, xiv, 118
co-creator, 152
collapse, xviii, xxviii, xxix, xxxii, xxxiii, xxxiv, xxxv, 121, 135, 166
commitment, 63, 68, 69, 71, 72, 73, 75, 76, 148
common-sense sacred axioms, 49
communion, xvi, xl, 27, 35, 39, 46, 47, 48, 101, 103, 164
community, xiv, 28, 67, 68, 72, 88, 101, 106, 113
complex, xviii, 16, 17, 102, 117, 120, 121, 129, 131, 165
complexity, xviii, 16, 30, 117, 151
complicated, xxxii, xxxvi, xxxviii, 127, 131
configuration, 8, 10, 15, 54, 55
Conscious Evolution, i, iii, iv, ix, x, xiii, xxii, xxiii, 3, 15, 19, 20, 26, 55, 79, 139, 140, 146, 147, 148, 149, 150, 153, 154, 156, 157, 158, 159, 160, 161, 162, 163, 164, 165, 167, 190, 191, 192
consciousness, xviii, xxi, xxii, xxiv, xxvi, xxx, 5, 6, 7, 14, 15, 16, 22, 26, 27, 31, 38, 39, 40, 42, 43, 47, 48, 50, 51, 56, 57, 58, 59, 60, 61, 62, 63, 64, 66, 68, 69, 70, 71, 73, 74, 75, 76, 82, 87, 99, 102, 103, 113, 136, 140, 142, 145, 149, 151, 155, 165, 190, 191
contemplating, 93

context for our diversity, xiii, xvi, xxxii, xl, 5, 9, 145
continuity of consciousness, xxx, 22, 26, 27, 31, 39, 40, 43, 47, 48, 50, 51, 87, 113, 145
contraction, 166
control, 17, 88, 117
convergence, 115, 191
conversation, xxiii, xxx, 5, 29, 38, 61, 62, 81, 85, 87, 96, 115, 118, 122, 123, 124, 126, 128, 131, 132, 133, 134, 154, 156, 157
cosmocentric, xviii, 7, 41, 94, 97
CosmoErotic Humanism, xiii, xvii, xviii, xxi, xxii, xxiii, xxix, xxxvii, xxxix, xl, 78, 97, 103, 106, 154, 190, 191
CosmoErotic Universe, xxii, 78
Cosmos, vi, xv, xvi, xviii, xxi, xxvii, xxix, xxxvii, 3, 10, 11, 13, 15, 44, 55, 56, 57, 59, 63, 66, 67, 78, 80, 97, 107, 133, 138, 155, 156, 164, 190
covenant, xxiv, 84
creating, 31, 82, 99, 100, 138
creation, xviii, xxii, xxiii, 11, 12, 16, 18, 19, 51, 98, 99, 100, 101, 102, 103, 114, 153
creative, xxiii, xxxi, xxxix, 80, 102, 133, 134, 135, 148, 151, 152, 160, 163
creativity, xxvi, 13, 19, 57, 70, 73, 84, 97, 99, 115, 135, 136, 137, 146, 152, 153, 164, 165
cultural, xv, xxxiii, xxxviii, xl, 60, 64

culture, xv, xviii, xxiv, xxvi, xxxi, xxxii, xxxvii, 17, 19, 20, 45, 62, 63, 74, 116, 117, 119, 127, 140, 150, 190, 191

D

daemon, 98, 126
death, xxx, xxxi, xxxii, xxxvii, 25, 26, 27, 29, 30, 31, 33, 36, 37, 38, 39, 41, 46, 48, 49, 51, 112, 113, 114, 142, 143, 159, 167
deepest heart's desire, 8, 13, 17, 18, 19, 20, 26
delight, 2, 15, 138, 146, 158, 164
desire, xxxiv, xl, 3, 8, 10, 12, 13, 15, 16, 17, 18, 19, 20, 26, 35, 46, 53, 54, 55, 66, 99, 139, 141, 161, 162
dignity, 4, 78, 82, 88, 91, 93, 94, 95, 97, 105, 131, 133, 134, 137, 138
diversity, xiii, xvi, xxxii, xl, 5, 9, 145
divides, xvi, 98, 126
Divine, 11, 18, 56, 83
dodee, 45
dofek, 45
dogma, xiv, xv, 10, 31, 57

E

Earth, xxviii, 15, 17, 59, 99, 149
Eastern, 90, 104
economics, xl, 11, 150
ecstasy, 75, 82, 107, 109
ego, 7, 30, 81, 89, 123, 125
egocentric, 7, 94, 97, 109
electron, 156
embodied, iv, 113
embracing, 105

emerge, 89, 90, 127, 142, 155
empire, 67, 69
emptiness, xxxiv, 142, 146, 147
emunah, 32
enlightenment, xl, 14, 39, 41, 45, 48, 54, 80, 92
Eros, xvii, xviii, xix, xxii, xxvii, xxviii, xxix, xxxiv, xxxvi, xxxviii, 8, 10, 15, 30, 42, 53, 78, 97, 101, 142, 157, 158, 162, 164, 190
erotic, xxxix, 53
et, 45
ethnocentric, xv, 7, 40, 41, 61, 93, 94, 97, 106, 109
ethos, xvi, xviii, 9, 29, 98, 126, 190
ever-deeper, xxix
ever-greater, xxix
evil, 61, 83
evolution, xv, xvi, xviii, xxii, xxiii, xxv, xxvi, xxvii, xxxi, xxxvii, xxxix, xl, 5, 8, 11, 20, 21, 22, 26, 27, 31, 53, 62, 78, 92, 94, 98, 99, 100, 101, 102, 103, 106, 112, 113, 114, 115, 122, 125, 134, 139, 140, 146, 148, 149, 150, 151, 152, 153, 154, 155, 156, 157, 158, 159, 161, 162, 163, 164, 165, 166, 191
of consciousness, xviii, xxi, xxiv, xxvi, xxx, 5, 6, 7, 14, 22, 26, 27, 31, 38, 39, 40, 43, 47, 48, 50, 51, 56, 58, 59, 60, 61, 63, 64, 66, 68, 69, 70, 71, 73, 75, 76, 82, 87, 113, 136, 140, 145, 151, 191
of love, xxv, xxvi, xxvii, xxviii, xxxix, xl, 7, 31, 53, 92, 94, 98, 99, 101, 106, 114, 126, 133, 135, 140

INDEX

Evolutionary
  chain, vi, vii, viii, ix, x, xiii, xiv, xx, xxi, xxiii, xxxvii, 2, 3, 11, 14, 19, 28, 30, 33, 35, 38, 53, 75, 77, 87, 97, 98, 99, 100, 101, 102, 103, 111, 114, 115, 119, 122, 123, 126, 128, 137, 145, 155, 157, 158, 159, 160, 165, 190
  Church, viii, xiii, xxiii, 2, 11, 35, 38, 62, 66, 70, 85, 86, 87, 98, 99, 100, 101, 102, 103, 105, 145, 160
  family, 5, 32, 73, 160, 166
  impulse, xxix, 8, 18, 19, 20, 26, 54, 55, 98, 99, 100, 101, 102, 103, 104, 137, 139, 152, 156, 164
  Love, vi, vii, viii, xiv, xx, xxiii, xxv, xxviii, xxxiii, xxxvii, xl, 3, 14, 15, 19, 21, 22, 28, 30, 33, 46, 75, 78, 82, 83, 85, 87, 91, 94, 95, 97, 101, 102, 103, 109, 114, 126, 128, 134, 138, 157, 158, 162, 169, 190
  Love Code, vi, vii, viii, xx, 33, 126
  Love Story, xxiii, xxxvii, xl, 82, 134, 138
  partners, xiv, 6, 118, 145
  sensemaking, 113, 128, 130
  spirituality, xxii, 11, 61, 77, 79, 80, 81, 87, 90, 92, 93, 94, 97, 103, 105, 115, 118, 119, 121, 122, 123, 130, 137, 145, 190
  Unique Self, vii, viii, xiv, xvii, xviii, xxii, xxiii, 3, 7, 10, 11, 14, 15, 19, 21, 28, 33, 34, 35, 36, 47, 48, 51, 55, 56, 59, 62, 64, 76, 78, 80, 81, 82, 89, 90, 95, 96, 98, 99, 102, 103, 104, 106, 123, 126, 137, 138, 139, 140, 145, 153, 154, 164, 190
existentialism, 141

existential risk, xxvi, xxx, xxxi, xxxiv, xxxv, xxxvi, xxxvii, xxxviii, xxxix, 9, 25, 28, 51, 54, 55, 77, 78, 81, 82, 93, 112, 114, 116, 117, 134, 135, 136, 142
expand, xxvii, 106
exterior sciences, xv, 31
Eye
  of humanity, xix, xxiii, xxxi, xxxii, 4, 19, 25, 26, 27, 37, 51, 88, 91, 93, 96, 99, 101, 113, 114, 117, 131, 133, 134, 142, 143, 157, 191
  of Spirit, 11, 38, 72, 156
  of Value, vii, ix, xiii, xiv, xv, xvi, xvii, xx, xxiv, xxv, xxvi, xxviii, xxxii, xxxiii, xxxv, xxxviii, xxxix, xl, 54, 78, 92, 109, 119, 126, 134, 135, 136, 140, 141, 148, 154, 157, 190
Eytan, 132

F

face, xxxv, 8, 11, 25, 31, 46, 54, 75, 117, 146, 169
fairness, 43, 44
faith, 157, 170
father, 32, 65
features, xx
feelings, 101
feminine, 6, 7, 8, 56, 59, 60, 61, 63, 71, 127, 141
field, xxxvi, xxxviii, 9, 46, 49, 57, 58, 63, 81, 82, 92, 99, 101, 102, 111
Field, viii, xv, xvi, xxxviii, 59, 75, 80, 89, 92, 104, 108, 133, 134
  of Value, vii, ix, xiii, xiv, xv, xvi, xvii, xx, xxiv, xxv, xxvi, xxviii, xxxii, xxxiii, xxxv, xxxviii, xxxix, xl,

54, 78, 92, 109, 119, 126, 134, 135, 136, 140, 141, 148, 154, 157, 190

first-person, xxi, xxxi, 48, 56

First Principles, ix, xv, xvi, xvii, xxi, xxiii, xxv, xxvi, xxix, xxx, xxxii, xxxv, xxxix, 29, 54, 55, 91, 98, 119, 120, 121, 126, 132, 134, 135, 141, 144, 147, 156, 162, 163, 164, 166, 190, 191

first shock of existence, xxx, xxxi, 112, 113

forgive, 86

four forces, 10, 57

freedom, 26, 73, 76, 102, 103, 151, 161, 163, 164, 165

fulfilment, 10, 34

fundamental, 5, 39, 40, 54, 55, 65, 106

fundamentalist, xxi, 165

G

gender, 6, 156

genes, xxiii, 15, 111, 112, 118, 146, 153

genius, xxiii, 3, 15, 20, 33, 99, 101, 111, 112, 118, 140, 146, 148, 151, 153

gifts, xix, xxiv, 137

Global, xxxv, xxxvii, xxxix, 191
 ethos, xvi, xviii, 9, 29, 98, 126, 190
 intimacy, xviii, xxvii, xxix, xxxiv, xxxv, xxxvi, xxxvii, xxxviii, xxxix, 11, 14, 15, 30, 37, 46, 54, 55, 94, 134, 158, 164, 165
 intimacy disorder, xviii, xxxiv, xxxv, xxxvi, xxxvii, xxxviii, xxxix, 37, 55

global ethos for a global civilization, 9, 29, 98, 126, 190

Goddess, 2, 8, 162

gorgeousness, 56

gotten, 16, 20, 85, 86, 130, 154, 162

grammar of value, xxxii, xxxv, xxxvi, xl, 5, 109, 119, 145, 162

greatness, 38, 127

ground, xiv, xv, xvi, xxx, xl, 29, 80, 86, 91, 92, 95, 98, 126, 190

H

Hallelujah, 11, 58, 59, 138, 170, 171

Hanukkah, 143

Hasidic, 107

have to, xvi, xxvi, xxvii, xxxix, 5, 16, 18, 20, 29, 31, 37, 54, 56, 59, 63, 66, 75, 76, 79, 83, 84, 85, 91, 94, 96, 106, 109, 125, 128, 133, 134, 151, 153, 157

heart, xxviii, xl, 8, 10, 13, 16, 17, 18, 19, 20, 26, 30, 31, 32, 101, 102, 108, 113, 124, 125, 127, 128, 130, 139, 140, 141, 145

HeartMath, 116

heaven, 25, 37, 40, 41, 43, 44, 45, 46, 47, 50, 51, 70, 108

Hebrew, 42, 60, 107, 108, 131
 wisdom, xiv, xvi, xviii, xxii, 44, 54, 60, 141

hero, 45, 46, 47, 63, 116, 120

holy and broken Hallelujah, 58, 138

Holy of Holies, xviii, 4, 38, 61, 62, 79, 95, 147, 162, 163

Homo amor, xiv, xxii, 3, 10, 15, 26, 32, 33, 45, 46, 71, 72, 86, 92, 94, 95, 109, 137, 144, 190

Homo Deus, 119
Homo sapiens, xiv, 10, 26, 32, 45, 71, 109, 137, 144, 190
Homo universalis, 3
honor, 16, 30, 38, 79, 80, 81, 92, 95, 97, 105, 111, 115, 122, 125, 126, 130, 137, 147, 158
human, xviii, xxii, xxviii, xxix, xxx, xxxi, xxxii, xxxiii, xxxiv, xxxvi, xxxviii, xl, 4, 7, 9, 10, 15, 16, 25, 26, 27, 30, 32, 33, 38, 39, 45, 47, 49, 51, 54, 55, 61, 63, 67, 68, 72, 78, 82, 83, 84, 88, 90, 91, 92, 93, 94, 97, 98, 100, 106, 108, 109, 112, 113, 119, 126, 131, 132, 133, 134, 137, 140, 141, 142, 143, 144, 149, 150, 154, 155, 156, 158, 161, 162, 165, 190
humanism, xvii, 97
humanity, xiv, xvii, xix, xxiii, xxxi, xxxii, 4, 15, 19, 25, 26, 27, 36, 37, 51, 88, 91, 92, 93, 96, 99, 101, 102, 109, 112, 113, 114, 117, 131, 133, 134, 137, 142, 143, 144, 149, 151, 157, 190, 191
humans, 17, 82

I

identified, xxxviii, 106, 149, 150
identify, 96, 150
identity, xvi, xxxiv, xxxvi, xxxvii, xxxviii, xl, 5, 9, 10, 15, 26, 33, 54, 81, 104, 141, 190
illusion, 29, 30, 50
imagination, 29, 30, 133
imagine, 18, 21, 34, 55, 59, 99, 124, 151, 163

immortality, 51
individual, xv, xxviii, xxxviii, 3, 9, 25, 27, 46, 47, 67, 82, 88, 90, 91, 93, 95, 96, 97, 105, 107, 108, 109, 113, 134, 152
individuals, xxxii, 87
individuation, 81
infinite, xxi, 91, 101, 102, 130, 131, 132, 133
Infinity of Intimacy, xxi, xxii, 11, 58, 107, 138
Infinity of Power, xxi, 138
influence, xxvii, 8, 89, 152
integrate, 56, 59, 73, 93, 94, 130, 147, 148
integrating, xl, 11, 94, 147
integration, 2, 6
integrity, xx, 44, 83, 106, 109, 148
interior sciences, xv, xxii, xxix, xxx, xxxix, xl, 56, 60, 114, 156
internet, xxxii, 20, 28, 36, 102, 126, 127, 128, 129
intimacy, xviii, xxvii, xxix, xxxiv, xxxv, xxxvi, xxxvii, xxxviii, xxxix, 11, 14, 15, 30, 37, 46, 54, 55, 94, 134, 158, 164, 165
intimate, xvi, xxi, xxxvi, xxxvii, xl, 33, 35, 39, 46, 48, 59, 65, 80, 87, 103, 164
Intimate Universe, xxii, xxxvii, 3, 13, 78, 164
irreducible, 47, 81, 82, 90, 91, 93, 96, 97, 105, 130, 131, 133, 134, 137, 138, 164
Israel, 132

J

Jerusalem, 79, 95
Jesus, 35
joining genes, xxiii, 15, 112, 118
joining genius, xxiii, 15, 112, 118, 148
joy, xiv, xxvi, 1, 4, 44, 55, 140, 145, 167
justice, 11, 43, 44, 45

K

kindness, 83, 84, 87, 88, 91, 97, 109, 133
king, 170
kiss, 86
knowledge, xviii, 101, 140
kol, 32

L

larger whole, 46, 132
leaders, xiii, 106
leadership, xiii, 62, 117, 144
leading, xvi, xxii, 12, 13, 108, 141, 190
line, 5, 6, 7, 74, 88, 141
lineage, xiii, xv, xviii, 32, 95, 96, 107, 108, 131, 160
lo, 32
longing, 18, 19, 20, 40, 41, 51
love, xvi, xx, xxiv, xxv, xxvi, xxvii, xxviii, xxxix, xl, 2, 3, 4, 6, 7, 8, 11, 13, 19, 28, 30, 31, 33, 34, 35, 36, 42, 43, 46, 50, 51, 53, 56, 57, 58, 61, 64, 71, 76, 79, 80, 81, 82, 85, 86, 87, 88, 91, 92, 94, 95, 96, 97, 98, 99, 101, 102, 103, 106, 114, 115, 123, 124, 125, 126, 127, 133, 134, 135, 136, 139, 140, 143, 145, 147, 151, 158, 159, 162, 166, 167, 169, 170, 171
Love, vi, vii, viii, xiv, xx, xxiii, xxv, xxviii, xxxiii, xxxvii, xl, 3, 14, 15, 19, 21, 22, 28, 30, 33, 46, 75, 78, 82, 83, 85, 87, 91, 94, 95, 97, 101, 102, 103, 109, 114, 126, 128, 134, 138, 157, 158, 162, 169, 190
  story, xxii, xxvi, xxxiii, xxxiv, xxxv, xxxvi, xxxviii, xxxix, xl, 2, 3, 5, 9, 10, 12, 14, 15, 16, 27, 28, 29, 34, 35, 36, 37, 46, 47, 51, 53, 54, 56, 63, 73, 78, 82, 91, 93, 94, 95, 97, 98, 106, 107, 109, 112, 116, 120, 125, 126, 128, 133, 134, 135, 136, 137, 141, 142, 143, 144, 145, 147, 148, 154, 156, 157, 158, 190
LoveIntelligence, xxvii, 33, 46, 155, 156

M

ma, 32
manifestation, 57
masculine, 5, 6, 7, 8
master, 107, 160
materialism, xxx, 31, 38
meditation, 18, 100, 104, 143
memory, xxxvii, xxxix, 42, 43, 129
meta-crisis, xiii, xiv, xvii, xxxiv, xxxix, 143, 191
metaphor, 26
MeToo, 127
mey, 32
mind, xxxi, 10, 38, 50, 100, 102, 104, 113, 128, 155

INDEX

miracle, 168
mitosis, 155, 165
model, 21, 71, 81, 96, 123, 125, 126
modern, xvi, xviii, xxviii, xxxvi, xxxviii, xl, 2, 54, 93, 94
Modernity, xxxiii, xxxiv, 93, 140
molecule, 155, 156
Moshe, 107
mother, 32, 60, 102, 153
multi-cell, 16
music, xx, 5, 40, 98, 170
mystery, xvi, 34, 62, 145, 164
Mystery School, 112
mystic, 38, 53
mysticism, 56, 104

N

namah, 171
neo-Darwinian, 154
neo-Darwinism, 141
new, xiii, xiv, xvi, xvii, xviii, xix, xx, xxi, xxiv, xxv, xxvi, xxxii, xxxiii, xxxiv, xxxv, xxxvii, xxxix, xl, 2, 3, 5, 6, 9, 10, 12, 15, 17, 20, 21, 26, 27, 28, 29, 30, 32, 33, 34, 39, 51, 53, 54, 62, 66, 69, 73, 75, 78, 88, 91, 92, 94, 95, 96, 97, 102, 103, 106, 109, 112, 123, 125, 128, 130, 135, 136, 137, 138, 140, 141, 143, 144, 145, 147, 148, 149, 150, 154, 155, 156, 157, 162, 163, 164, 190, 191
New Age, 63, 70
new human, 15, 26, 32, 33, 51, 88, 91, 92, 109, 137, 143, 144, 190
new humanity, xiv, 15, 88, 92, 109, 137, 143, 144, 190
new Story, xiii, xiv, xvi, xvii, xviii, xx, xxiv, xxv, xxvi, xxxii, xxxiii, xxxix, xl, 54, 78, 109, 135, 136, 140, 141, 148, 154, 157
noosphere, 90, 91, 95, 102
Normandy, 47

O

obligation, 69
om, 171
ontological, xxx, 40, 41, 43, 48
Outrageous Acts of Love, 91
Outrageous Love, xiv, xx, xxiii, xxviii, xl, 3, 21, 28, 30, 75, 83, 109
Outrageous Love Story, xl

P

pandemic, xxxii, 4, 5, 54, 140
pan-interiority, xxx, 38
paradox, 81, 125
partial, 162
particular, xxix, 30, 53, 64, 66, 67, 69, 70, 71, 72, 74, 77, 79, 80, 81, 85, 88, 90, 108, 114, 123, 124, 127, 128, 129, 142, 143
pattern, 16, 33
Pentecost, xxiii, 51
Personhood of Cosmos, vi, xxi
physiosphere, 156
pi, 32
planetary awakening in love, 19, 28, 34, 35, 36, 51, 99, 102, 103
pleasure, 22, 97
plotline, 47, 113, 128, 129
postmodern, xvi, xl, 2, 54, 68, 93, 94, 119, 120, 121, 128, 130, 163

power, xix, xxix, xxxiv, xl, 33, 35, 66, 68, 73, 100, 108, 112, 114, 136, 141, 146, 167
prayer, xx, xxi, 10, 22, 34, 58, 65, 98, 99, 102, 107, 108, 138
premodern, xvi, 2, 40, 54, 93, 94, 112, 163
priest, 35
process, xv, xix, xx, 16, 78, 100, 102, 103, 118, 136, 151, 155, 156, 157, 161, 163, 164, 165
promise, 2, 126
proton, 156
psychology, xxviii
purpose, xxxvi, xxxvii, 7, 34, 56, 59, 60, 101, 102, 118, 152, 160

Q

quantum, 150, 191

R

radical, vi, xxix, 1, 7, 30, 32, 42, 51, 55, 63, 72, 75, 76, 147, 155, 161, 163, 165
Rama, 59
Ramadan, 143
Reality, vii, viii, xv, xviii, xxi, xxii, xxvi, xxix, xxxiv, xxxvi, xxxviii, xxxix, xl, 3, 4, 8, 13, 14, 15, 26, 29, 30, 31, 33, 36, 38, 39, 40, 42, 44, 47, 51, 53, 54, 56, 57, 59, 60, 70, 75, 82, 83, 90, 97, 108, 113, 137, 141, 142, 143, 160, 161, 164, 165
realization, xv, xviii, xxi, xxii, xxix, xxx, xxxi, xxxix, 3, 10, 13, 25, 26, 31, 44, 45, 54, 57, 58, 60, 80, 81, 102, 104, 134, 157, 160, 162, 164, 167
reflect, xxiii, 61
reincarnation, 38
relationship, iii, 29, 38, 61, 78, 112, 141, 159
religion, xxxiii, xl, 37, 64, 67, 69, 72, 144, 145, 151, 190
Renaissance, xxv, xxxii, 27, 28, 33, 37, 67, 112, 114, 140
resonance, xxxv, 102
resurrection, 26, 29, 30, 31, 33, 35, 37, 48
revealed, 127
Roman Empire, 66, 67
roshi, 43

S

sacred, 49, 102, 114, 160
sacrifice, 46, 63, 64, 70, 73, 74, 76
Saving Private Ryan, 46
second-person, 57
second shock of existence, xxx, xxxi, xxxii, 25, 26, 37, 51, 112, 113
security, 30, 100
Self, vii, viii, xiv, xvii, xviii, xxii, xxiii, xxix, 3, 7, 10, 11, 14, 15, 19, 21, 28, 33, 34, 35, 36, 39, 42, 45, 47, 48, 51, 55, 56, 59, 62, 64, 76, 78, 79, 80, 81, 82, 89, 90, 95, 96, 98, 99, 102, 103, 104, 106, 108, 122, 123, 126, 137, 138, 140, 145, 153, 154, 164, 171, 190
organizing, 28, 140
reflective, 149, 155
sensemaking, 113, 128, 130

separate self, 9, 14, 26, 67, 80, 89, 104
separation, 100, 101
service, 1, 26, 75, 76, 149, 153
sexual, 53
sexuality, 18
shadow, 87, 105, 115, 118, 119
Shakti, 59
shiva, 171
shivaya, 171
shock of existence, xxx, xxxi, xxxii, 25, 26, 37, 51, 112, 113
social construction, 142
Solomon, xviii, xxii, 43, 45, 97
Song of Songs, 21
soul, 163, 168, 171
Source, 17, 18, 19, 141, 144
source code, xviii, xxiv, xxvi, 62, 63, 73, 74, 113, 114, 115, 128, 190, 191
Spiral Dynamics, 64
Spirit, 11, 38, 39, 72, 99, 156
story, xxii, xxvi, xxxiii, xxxiv, xxxv, xxxvi, xxxviii, xxxix, xl, 2, 3, 5, 9, 10, 12, 14, 15, 16, 27, 28, 29, 34, 35, 36, 37, 46, 47, 51, 53, 54, 56, 63, 73, 78, 82, 91, 93, 94, 95, 97, 98, 106, 107, 109, 112, 116, 120, 125, 126, 128, 133, 134, 135, 136, 137, 141, 142, 143, 144, 145, 147, 148, 154, 156, 157, 158, 190
Story of Value, vii, ix, xiii, xiv, xv, xvi, xvii, xx, xxiv, xxv, xxvi, xxviii, xxxii, xxxiii, xxxv, xxxviii, xxxix, xl, 54, 78, 109, 119, 126, 135, 136, 140, 141, 148, 154, 157
St. Paul, 34, 36
structures, 3, 9, 63
synagogue, 75, 145
synergy, xiv, xxiii, 12, 13, 19, 115, 151, 152, 161, 163

T

tachat, 43
Tao, xv, 31, 37
Tao, the, 31
tat, 57
techno-optimist, 91, 93
telos, 156, 161, 163
temple, 79, 95
tenderness, 92
Thanos, 93, 116, 117, 118, 119, 120, 121, 131, 134, 136
the Now, 112
the One, xiv, xxi, xxvii, 79, 161
the Universe, xv, xxiii, 3, 16, 37, 47, 56, 78, 82, 94, 106, 134, 138, 152, 153, 154, 156
The Universe
   A Love Story, xxxvii, 138
The whole, 149
third-person, xxi, 10, 56
totalitarianism, 89, 90, 91, 92, 103, 104, 105
traditions, xiv, xv, xviii, xxii, 14, 93, 107, 131
tragic, xiv, 88, 96, 120, 125, 127
transcend, iii, 22, 46
transformation, xvi, xvii, xxix, 49, 118, 122, 137, 143, 150, 164
transmission, xvii, xix, xx, 61
tribe, 65, 66, 67, 69, 70, 72
True Self, 14, 15, 42, 89, 104, 108

truth, xxvi, xxviii, xl, 26, 29, 40, 41, 48, 50, 51, 79, 97, 116, 124, 128, 168, 171
tvam, 57

U

uncertainty, 50
unconscious, xxii, 146
understanding, xix, 38, 40, 62, 105, 124, 132, 140, 141, 154, 155, 158, 161, 165
unique gender, 6
unique gift, 10, 14, 19, 48, 99, 102, 153, 154
unique intimacy, 54, 55
uniqueness, xvi, 7, 13, 14, 19, 47, 48, 81, 105, 133, 134, 164, 165
Unique Self, vii, viii, xiv, xvii, xviii, xxii, xxiii, 3, 7, 10, 11, 14, 15, 19, 21, 28, 33, 34, 35, 36, 47, 48, 51, 55, 56, 59, 62, 64, 76, 78, 80, 81, 82, 89, 90, 95, 96, 98, 99, 102, 103, 104, 106, 123, 126, 137, 138, 139, 140, 145, 153, 154, 164, 190
Unique Self Symphony, xviii, 3, 7, 14, 19, 21, 33, 35, 36, 55, 56, 59, 62, 76, 78, 98, 99, 102, 103, 106, 126, 138, 140, 145, 164
unique voice, 99
universal grammar of value, xxxii, 5, 109, 145, 162
Universe, xv, xvi, xxii, xxiii, xxx, xxxiii, xxxiv, xxxvii, 3, 13, 14, 15, 16, 37, 46, 47, 56, 78, 82, 94, 95, 106, 134, 138, 141, 152, 153, 154, 156, 164, 190

Universe Story, xvi, xxxiii, xxxiv, 190
utopia, xxxii, 25, 73, 82, 89, 108, 137

V

values, xiv, xv, xxxiv, xxxv, xxxviii, xxxix, 6, 7, 56, 59, 60, 61, 63, 65, 68, 71, 120, 132, 162, 164, 165
via, 122
visionary, 190
viymino, 43
vocation, 99, 101, 152, 153
voice, xxiii, 35, 36, 45, 57, 90, 99, 102, 103, 108, 112, 146, 191

W

wake, xxxviii, 55, 56, 59, 60, 62, 63, 72, 76, 149
watch, 6, 21, 117
Western, 56, 67, 75, 104
Western Enlightenment, 67
Wheel of Co-Creation, vi, ix, 4, 8, 9, 10, 11, 12, 15, 18, 19, 54, 115, 191
where we are, 109
whole mate, iii, 53, 159, 166, 167
whole, the, 47
who we are, 28, 98, 109, 127
win/lose, xviii, xxvi, xxvii, xxxi, xxxii, xxxiv, xxxvi, xxxviii, 7, 9, 26

Y

yearning, 19, 51
yoga, 144

yom, 32
Yom Kippur, 108

Z

Zuboff, Shoshana, 28, 89

ABOUT THE AUTHORS

Dr. Marc Gafni is a visionary world philosopher and futurist, one of the leading formulators of world spirituality and religion of our time, and a beloved teacher and public intellectual. He holds his doctorate in philosophy from Oxford University, as well as Orthodox rabbinic ordination. He co-founded the activist think tank, now called the Center for World Philosophy and Religion, where he serves as the co-president with Dr. Zachary Stein. He also served with Barbara Marx Hubbard as co-president of the Foundation for Conscious Evolution, which he consented to lead at Barbara's request after her passing.

He is known for his "source code teachings"—including Unique Self theory and the Five Selves, the Amorous Cosmos, a Politics of Evolutionary Love, a Return to Eros, and Digital Intimacy—and has more than twenty books to his name, including the award-winning Your Unique Self, A Return to Eros, and three volumes of Radical Kabbalah.

He teaches on the cutting edge of philosophy in the West, helping to evolve a new *dharma* or meta-theory of Integral meaning that is helping to reshape key pivoting points in global consciousness and culture, with the aim of participating in the articulation of what Dr. Gafni and Dr. Stein, along with other colleagues, are calling CosmoErotic Humanism.

At the core of CosmoErotic Humanism is what Dr. Gafni and Dr. Stein are calling First Principles and First Values, Anthro-Ontology, and a Universal Grammar of Value. This is the ground of a new shared Universe Story and a new narrative of identity for the new human and the new humanity. This is what they are calling the emergence from *Homo sapiens* to *Homo amor*. This shared story rooted in First Principles and First Values can then serve as the matrix for a global ethos for a global civilization.

Together with Dr. Stein and Ken Wilber, Gafni is writing a series of seminal books under the collective pseudonym of David J. Temple, which intend to evolve the source code of consciousness and culture in response to the meta-crisis. The first of those books is *First Principles and First Values: Forty-Two Propositions on CosmoErotic Humanism, the Meta-Crisis, and the World to Come.*

Barbara Marx Hubbard (born Barbara Marx; December 22, 1929–April 10, 2019) was an American futurist, author, and public speaker. She is credited with the Wheel of Co-Creation, and together with Dr. Gafni, the Wheel of Co-Creation 2.0, as well as the concepts of the Synergy Engine and the "birthing" of humanity.

As co-founder and president of the Foundation for Conscious Evolution and the chair, for the last five years of her life, of the Center for World Philosophy and Religion, she posited that humanity was on the threshold of a quantum leap if newly emergent scientific, social, and spiritual capacities were integrated to address global crises.

She was the author of seven books on social and planetary evolution. In conjunction with the Shift Network, she co-produced the worldwide "Birth 2012" multimedia event. She was also the subject of a biography by author Neale Donald Walsch, *The Mother of Invention: The Legacy of Barbara Marx Hubbard*. Deepak Chopra called her "the voice for conscious evolution."

In 1984, she was symbolically nominated for the vice presidency of the United States. She also co-chaired a number of Soviet-American Citizen Summits, introducing a new concept called SYNCON, to foster synergistic convergence with opposing groups. In addition, she co-founded the World Future Society and the Association for Global New Thought.

VOLUME 16 — *The Next Step in Conscious Evolution*

LIST OF EPISODES

1. Episode 219 — December 20, 2020

2. Episode 234 — April 4, 2021

3. Episode 263 — October 24, 2021

4. Episode 300 — July 10, 2022

5. Episode 301 — July 17, 2022

6. Episode 323 — December 18, 2022

7. Episode 392 — April 14, 2024

www.ingramcontent.com/pod-product-compliance
Lightning Source LLC
LaVergne TN
LVHW011153080426
835508LV00007B/369